DORSET AND SOMERSET NARROW GAUGE

Vic Mitchell and Keith Smith

MP Middleton Press

Cover pictures:
   Front upper - Dorset was noted for its clay carrying railways and Peckett 0-4-2ST Septimus was recorded in September 1951 with ball clay for Pike Bros. Works at Furzebrook. (F.Jones/RMC coll.)
   Front lower - Somerset has a notable two-foot gauge pleasure line near Templecombe. Part of its northern terminus was photographed in its infancy in August 1991. (P.G.Barnes)

   Back lower - Authors Keith Smith (left) and Vic Mitchell squat beside no. 2 Northern Chief *at Hythe on 16th May 1999, prior to its departure with the 1.00pm book launch train for their* Romneyrail *album (P.G.Barnes)*

ACKNOWLEDGEMENTS

We are very grateful for the assistance received from many of those mentioned in the credits also to M.Bowditch, A.R.Carder, R.S.Carpenter, F.Holland, J.B.Horne, N.Langridge, Mr D. and Dr S.Salter, J.Watts and particularly our ever supportive wives, Barbara Mitchell and Janet Smith.

Published May 2006

ISBN 1 904474 76 4

Design Deborah Esher
Typesetting Barbara Mitchell

Published by
            Middleton Press
            Easebourne Lane
            Midhurst, West Sussex
            GU29 9AZ
Tel: 01730 813169
Fax: 01730 812601
Email: info@middletonpress.co.uk
www.middletonpress.co.uk

Printed & bound by Biddles Ltd, Kings Lynn

SECTIONS

Dorset		Somerset	
1	Industry	4	Industry
2	Military	5	Pleasure
3	Pleasure		

CONTENTS

Industry and Military Lines

The diagrams show pre-1974 county boundaries and the approximate location of the first photograph in each sequence.

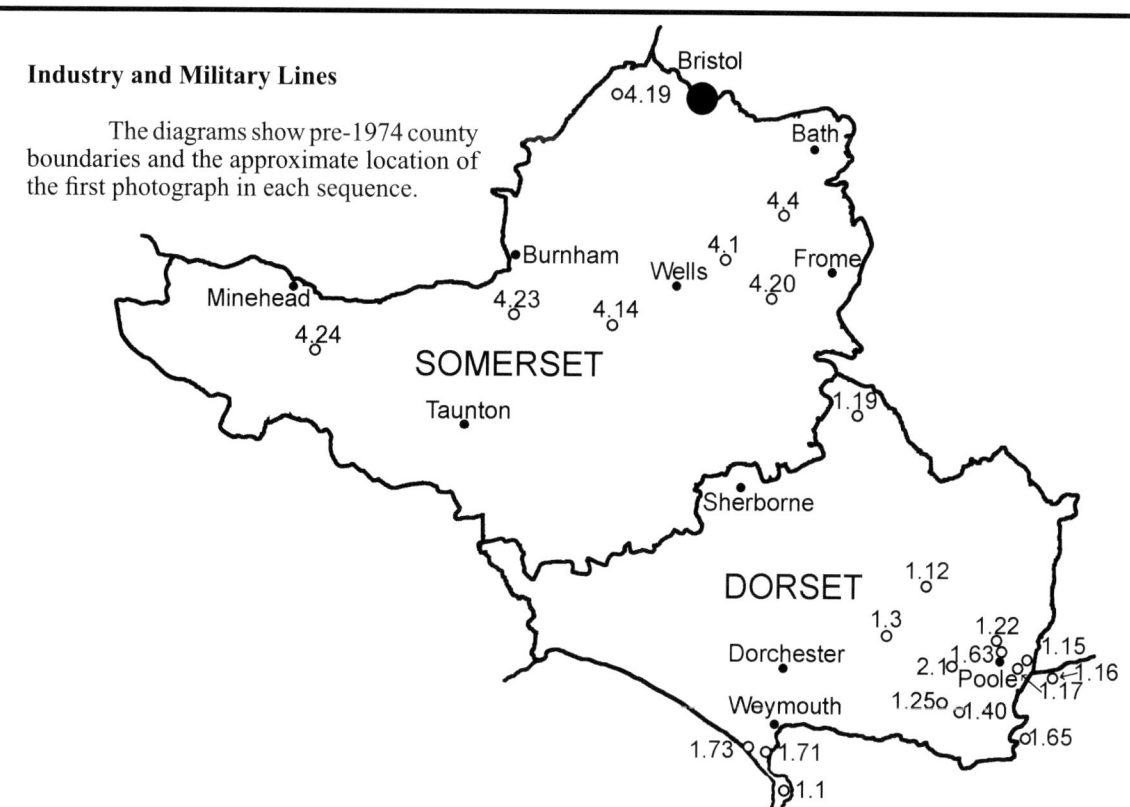

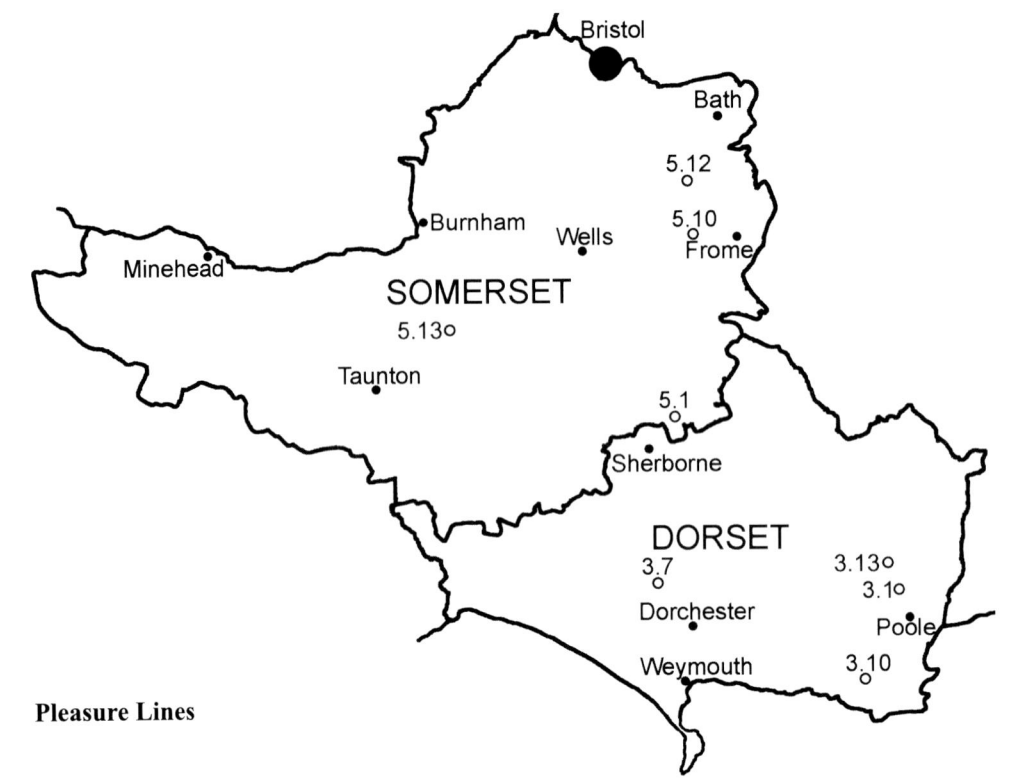

Bristol

Bath
•

5.12
○

5.10
○
Frome •

•Burnham

Wells
•

Minehead
•

SOMERSET

5.13○

Taunton
•

5.1
○

Sherborne
•

DORSET

3.7
○

3.13○
3.1○

Dorchester
•

Poole
•

Weymouth
•

3.10
○

Pleasure Lines

INTRODUCTION

Despite the fine netting on our trawl, we have been unable to find illustrations of the following lines:

Dorset
Binegar Pits
Brickhill Brickworks at Bedlam
Decca Record Co. Ltd at Holton Heath
Hine Bros (Ringwood) Ltd at Gillingham Pits
Omnium Manufacturers Ltd at Mannings Brickfields, Parkstone
Royal Navy Underwater Weapons Establishment at Bincleaves near Weymouth
Sykes & Son (Poole) Ltd at Creekmoor Potteries

Somerset
Colthurst Symons & Co. Ltd at Burnham-on-Sea and Bridgwater
Moorewood Colliery at Oakhill
Roads Reconstruction (1934) Ltd at -
    Emborough Quarry
    Vallis Vale Quarry
    Vobster Limestone Quarry
Royal Ordnance Factory, Huntspill at Puriton
Somerset Quarry Co. Ltd at Frome
Somerset Rivers Catchment Board at Bradney
Somerset Trading Co. at Bridgwater Brickworks
Western Trinidad Lake Asphalt Co. Ltd at Leigh-on-Mendip
John Browne & Co. (Bridgwater) Ltd at Chilton Trinity
Laporte Industries at Combe Hay Quarry
William Thomas & Co. Ltd at Wellington
E.J.Godwin (Peat Industries) Ltd at Meare

1. Industry - Dorset

F.J.BARNES LTD
PORTLAND QUARRIES

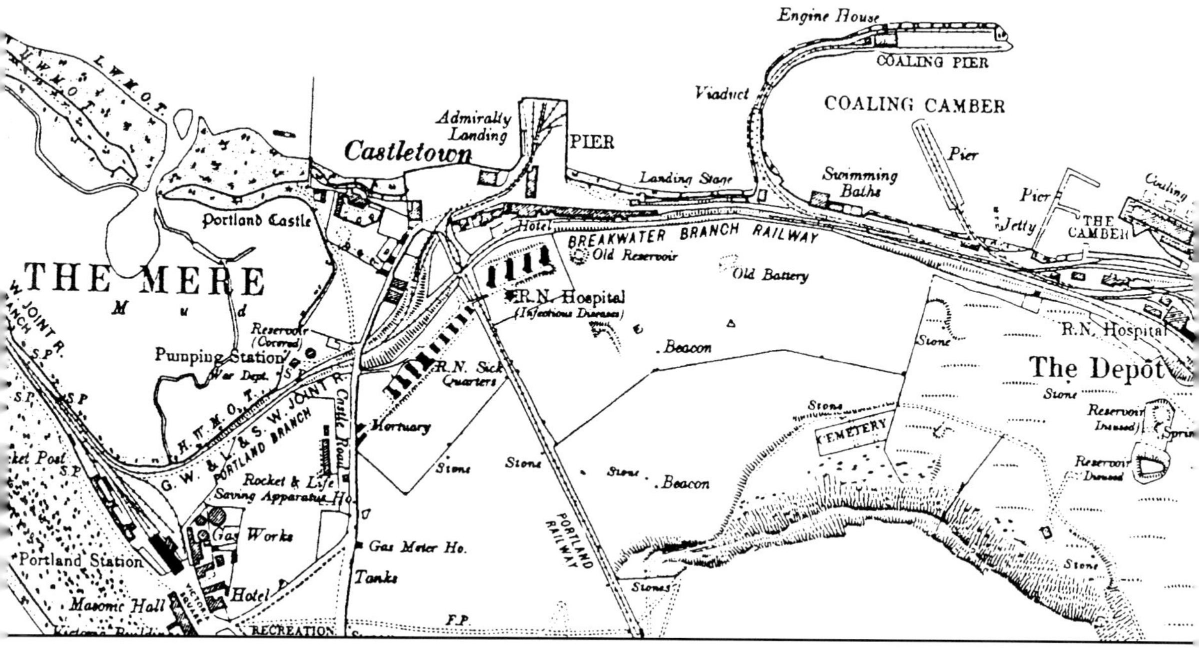

The 4ft 6ins gauge Portland Railway is lower centre on this 1903 map at 6ins to 1 mile. The Weymouth to Easton line runs across it and also the centre of the next picture. The Castletown Pier was used for the despatch of stone from its north and east faces.

1.1   This southward view includes Freeman's Incline and the motive power for finished stone products. The line was in use from 1826 to 1939 and was 4ft 6ins gauge. (Weymouth Local History Museum)

1.2   On the upper levels, steam was used for waste disposal, but the track gauge was two feet. The 0-4-2T *Excelsior* was built by W.G.Bagnall Ltd with an inverted saddle tank in 1888 and was purchased from James Nuttall & Sons in 1898. (Weymouth Local History Museum)

BEDFORD & JESTY LTD
BERE REGIS

1.3   Six miles northwest of Wareham is one of the largest producers of watercress. The first photographs date from September 1967 and give an impression of the extent of the 18ins trackwork. We start our tour at the warehouse. (P.Nicholson)

1.4   Unusual for a watercress railway, the terrain traversed is not entirely flat and few can claim to have a bridge. The site is known as Doddings Farm and is near Bedlam, but not the one famed for disorder, which is in Kent. (P.Nicholson)

1.5   The firm's trade name was promoted on its locomotive, which was built in Dorchester in 1948 by B.J.Fry. It was powered by an Austin 7 engine. (P.Nicholson)

1.6   Not only was the line provided with an overbridge, but a viaduct was also constructed. The sole passenger vehicle is seen again. The farm is private and not open to the public. (P.Nicholson)

1.7   The platform in the washing shed was recorded on 4th June 1969. The spring water flows into the Bere Stream, which discharges into the River Piddle. (M.A.N.Johnston)

1.8   Part of the main line was photographed on the same day, along with a reserve of gravel, which was conveyed by rail in skips for maintenance of the beds. (M.A.N.Johnston)

1.9   A photograph from August 1972 features a model built at the Regent Street Polytechnic School of Engineering and reboilered in 1967. It was then owned by Mr R.G.Pratt and arrived here in 1970. It is seen unlined, the first steaming being in June 1973. It received GNR lettering and was sold about four months later. (J.K.Williams coll.)

1.10   Refuelling was recorded in mid-journey on 24th April 1973. The petrol power unit was manufactured in 1933, but the watercress beds were created in the 1880s. (C.G.Maggs)

1.11   An abundant harvest was photographed on the same day, fresh water from chalk springs being essential for watercress growth. About 130 tons are produced annually on this site, but only a short section of the track was in use in 2006 and the trucks were then hand propelled. (C.G.Maggs)

BEDFORD & JESTY LTD SPETISBURY

1.12 Ten miles north of Wareham is the village of Spetisbury, which was spelt Spettisbury until the mid-20th century. This group of photographs was taken in 1970-75. The gauge was two feet, but no trace of the railway now remains. (P.Nicholson)

1.13 Few railway bridges are as low as this one in the Stour Valley. A chalk spring feeds the beds, the water then flowing into the River Stour. Bedford & Jesty Ltd was purchased by Vitacress Salads Ltd in 1980. (P.Nicholson)

1.14 This farm is one of ten in Dorset and Hampshire owned by Vitacress Salads Ltd. This one also produces about 130 tons of watercress each year. A motorised trolley served as farm transport for many years, until line closure in about 1980. The village had another railway until 1966; it was the Somerset & Dorset line. The station had become a halt in 1934. (P.Nicholson)

BOURNEMOUTH GAS &
WATER COMPANY

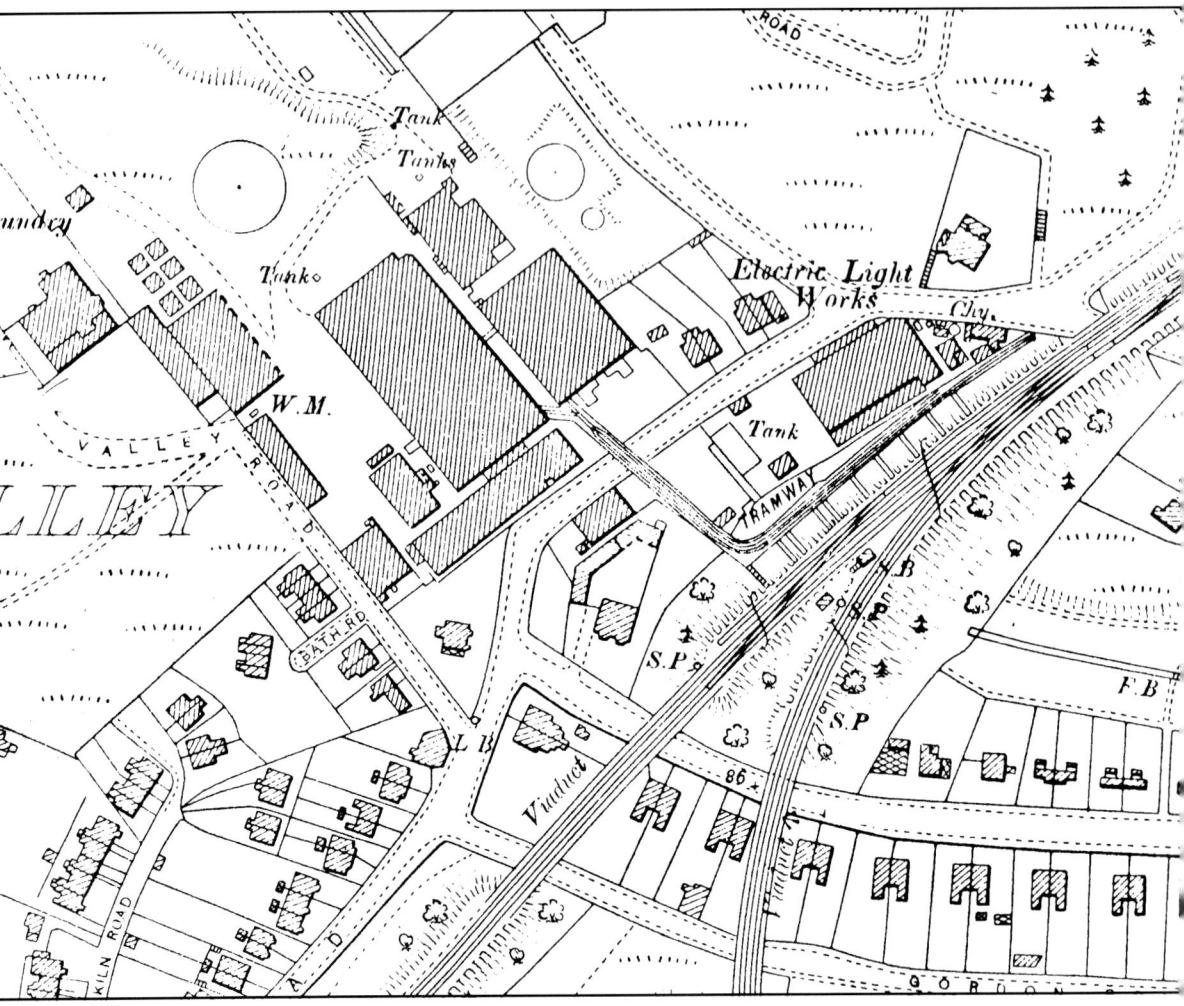

The works was built in 1862-64 near to the junction of the branch to Bournemouth West, which is curving at the bottom of this 1937 map at 25 ins to 1 mile. The private siding had timber chutes into which coal was shovelled into wagons below. Their gauge was about 3ft and they were hand propelled to the coal store. The route, which was almost all elevated, included a spindly cast-iron viaduct over a public road. When the Electricity Works was built at the foot of the embankment, the tramway was extended north into its coal stores. Additional coal chutes were built at the same time, about 1900. The Gas Company was growing too rapidly for the Bourne Valley site and in 1902 bought the much older Poole gasworks, not just to enlarge their district, but because the Poole works had access to deep water, where colliers from the North East could discharge. Gasmaking was transferred to Poole, where some very innovative plant was installed; Bourne Valley last made gas in 1918, but it remains an important holder station to this day.

1.15   The narrow gauge had a final fling at Bourne Valley in about 1930, when a large gasholder was built. A great deal of sand and clay had to be moved before the holder's foundation raft could be laid. Vale, the contractor, used a dragline excavator which loaded the spoil into two-foot gauge side-tipping skips. Two Simplex locos were used. (Southern Gas Board)

BOURNEMOUTH PIER

1.16   Major maintenance work was required in 1980 and a two-foot gauge line was used by Christiani & Nielson. This was one of Dorset's transitory railways. (P.Nicholson)

GEORGE JENNINGS,
SOUTH WESTERN POTTERY
PARKSTONE

The standard gauge private siding from Parkstone station is at the top of this 1937 edition at 25ins to 1 mile. The connection to the Southern Railway is shown in our *Bournemouth to Weymouth* album. The two-foot gauge line runs between the clay pit and the pottery. Lower left is a fenced curve, which once took a standard gauge track to Salterns Pier.

Clay Pit

Engine Shed

MINERAL RAILWAY

Pumping House

Chy.

Kiln

Engine House

South Wes Pottery

Chy.

Kilns

Chy.

Kiln

W.M.

Kilns

Clay Pit

Lave

C.R.

1.17   The pottery was opened in 1856 and Salterns Pier followed in 1867. The line from Parkstone station opened in 1874, but the track to the pier fell into disuse in about 1925. The routes were changed over the years and so this 1963 photograph does not correspond with the map. (M.A.N.Johnston)

1.18   Hibberd Planet no. 3790 of 1956 was recorded with clay from the pit on 30th April 1957. Drainage pipes were the main product of the pottery, but demand declined as the plastics industry expanded and closure took place in about 1963. (A.Attewell)

Cheese Factory

GILLINGHAM POTTERY,
BRICK & TILE CO. LTD

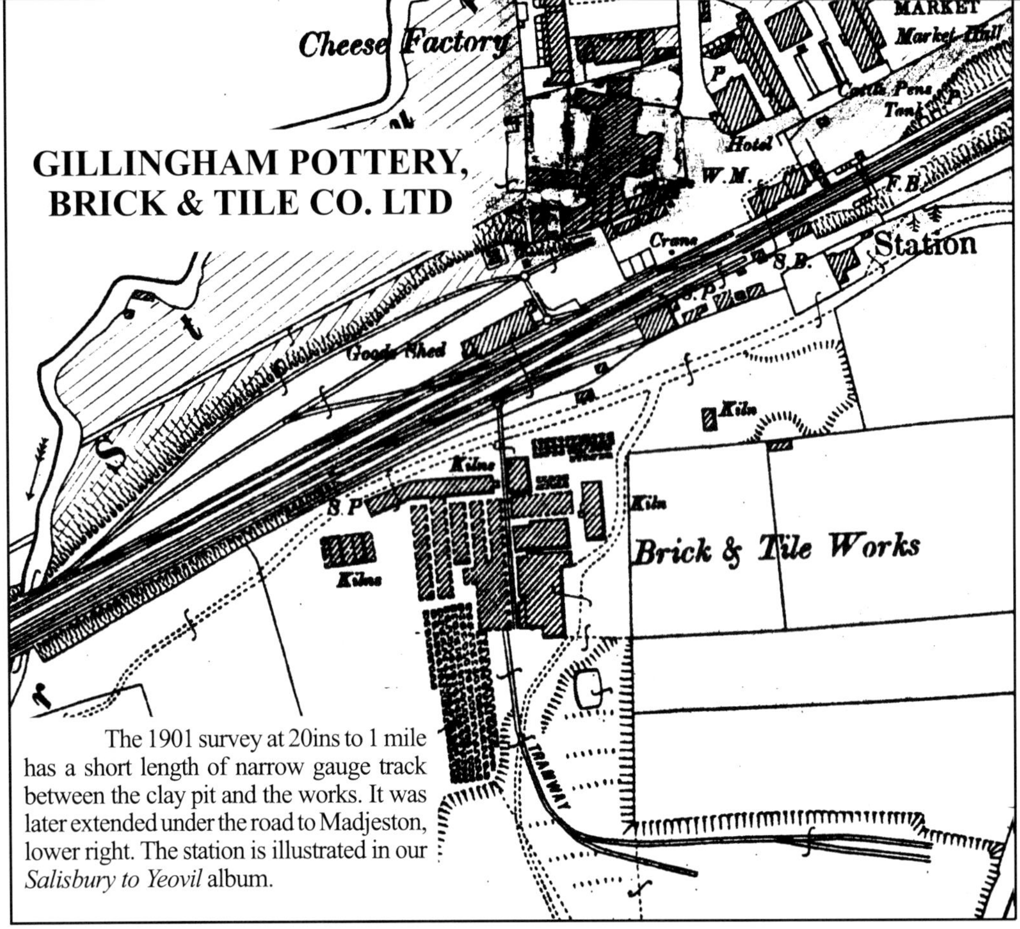

Market
Market Hall
Cattle Pens
Tank
Hotel
W.M.
F.B.
Crane
Station
S.B.
Goods Shed
Kiln
Kiln
S.P.
Kilns
Kiln
Kilns
Brick & Tile Works
TRAMWAY

The 1901 survey at 20ins to 1 mile has a short length of narrow gauge track between the clay pit and the works. It was later extended under the road to Madjeston, lower right. The station is illustrated in our *Salisbury to Yeovil* album.

1.19   The works seems to have been established about six years after the main line opened in 1859; this brought coal cheaply. It seems that mechanisation did not take place until the 1930s. Seen in March 1966 is the loading equipment at the pit. (P.Henshaw)

1.20 The works end of the line was recorded at the same time, in poor weather. A steel rope was used to haul the wagons up the incline on the left. The gauge was two feet. (P.Henshaw)

1.21 The works was dismantled in 1970 and this photograph from February 1971 shows the locos prior to removal for preservation; all three were saved. Here is Ruston & Hornsby no. 189972, plus part of Motor Rail no. 2059 of 1920. Drain pipes are evident, part of the final production run. The site became an industrial estate and the pit a fishing lake. (P.Nicholson)

LYTCHETT BRICK CO. LTD
UPTON

1.22   The clay pit was photographed on 15th July 1966. The reach of the face shovel limited trains to two wagons. The works was situated north of Upton Parish Church, which was on the old A35.(P.Henshaw)

1.23   A closer look at the locomotive on the same day shows the inclined exhaust pipe. This position prevented fumes collecting under the roof over the discharge pit, seen in the next picture. The loco is 4WD Ruston & Hornsby no. 178990 of 1936. (P.Henshaw)

1.24   An April 1964 photograph shows the pit from which the clay was taken by aerial ropeway to the works. The area is now covered with housing. This is another Ruston & Hornsby product. (P.Henshaw)

The 1901 map at 25 ins to 1 mile shows the private siding from the LSWR's line between Broadstone and Hamworthy, the original route from Southampton to Weymouth. The works tramway was lengthened and repositioned in later years. The gauge was two feet.

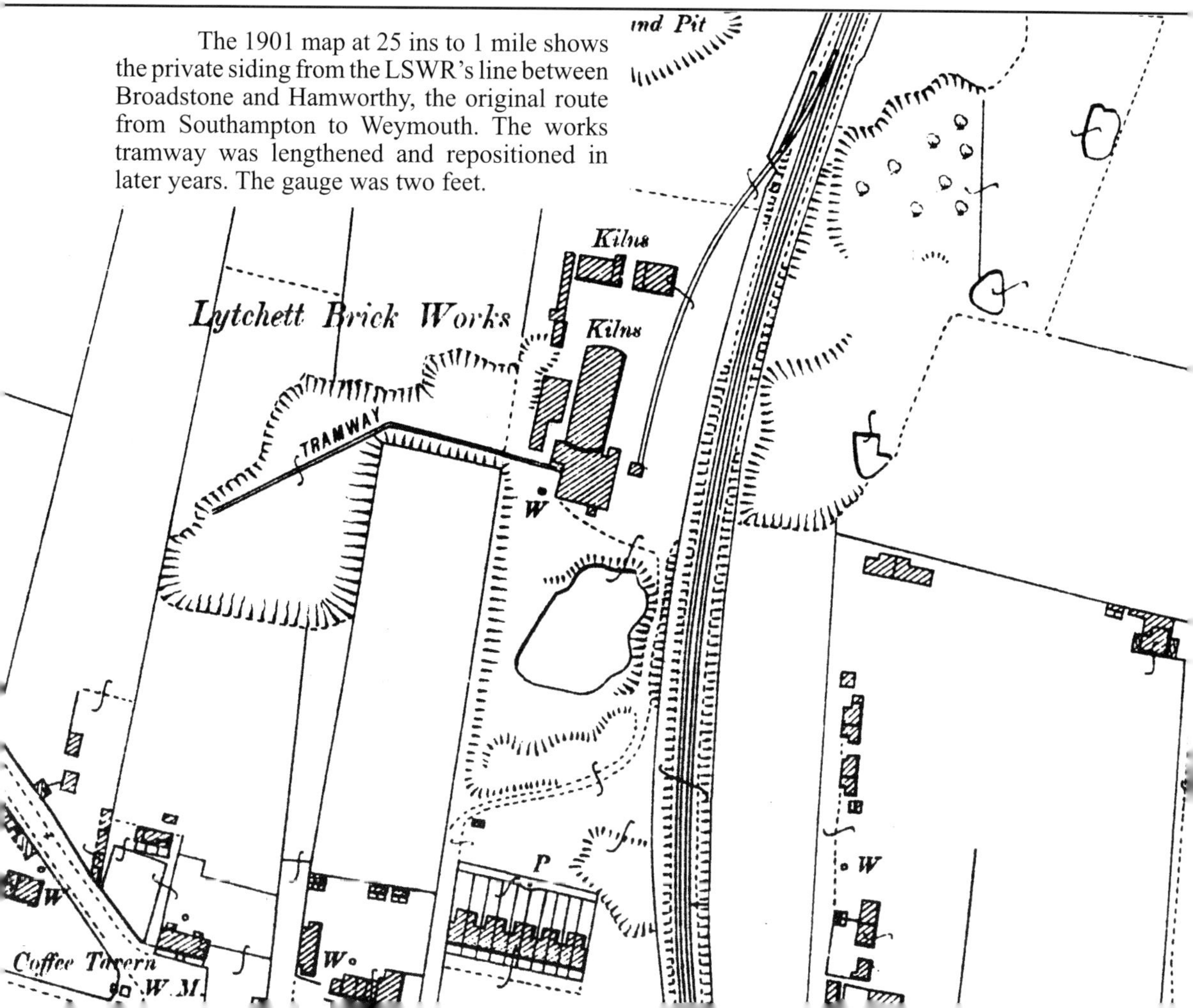

nd Pit

Kilns

Lytchett Brick Works

Kilns

TRAMWAY

Coffee Tavern

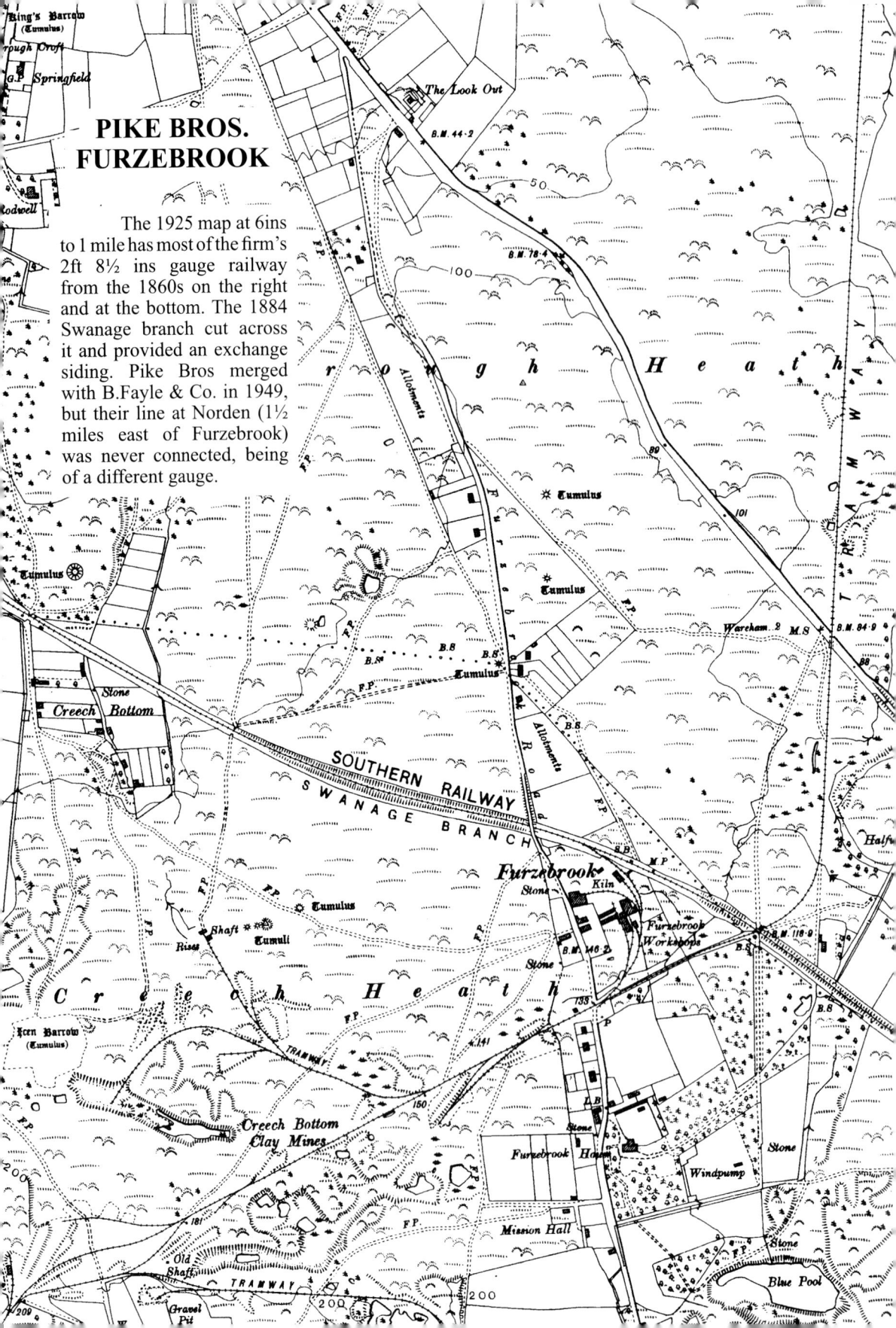

PIKE BROS.
FURZEBROOK

The 1925 map at 6ins to 1 mile has most of the firm's 2ft 8½ ins gauge railway from the 1860s on the right and at the bottom. The 1884 Swanage branch cut across it and provided an exchange siding. Pike Bros merged with B.Fayle & Co. in 1949, but their line at Norden (1½ miles east of Furzebrook) was never connected, being of a different gauge.

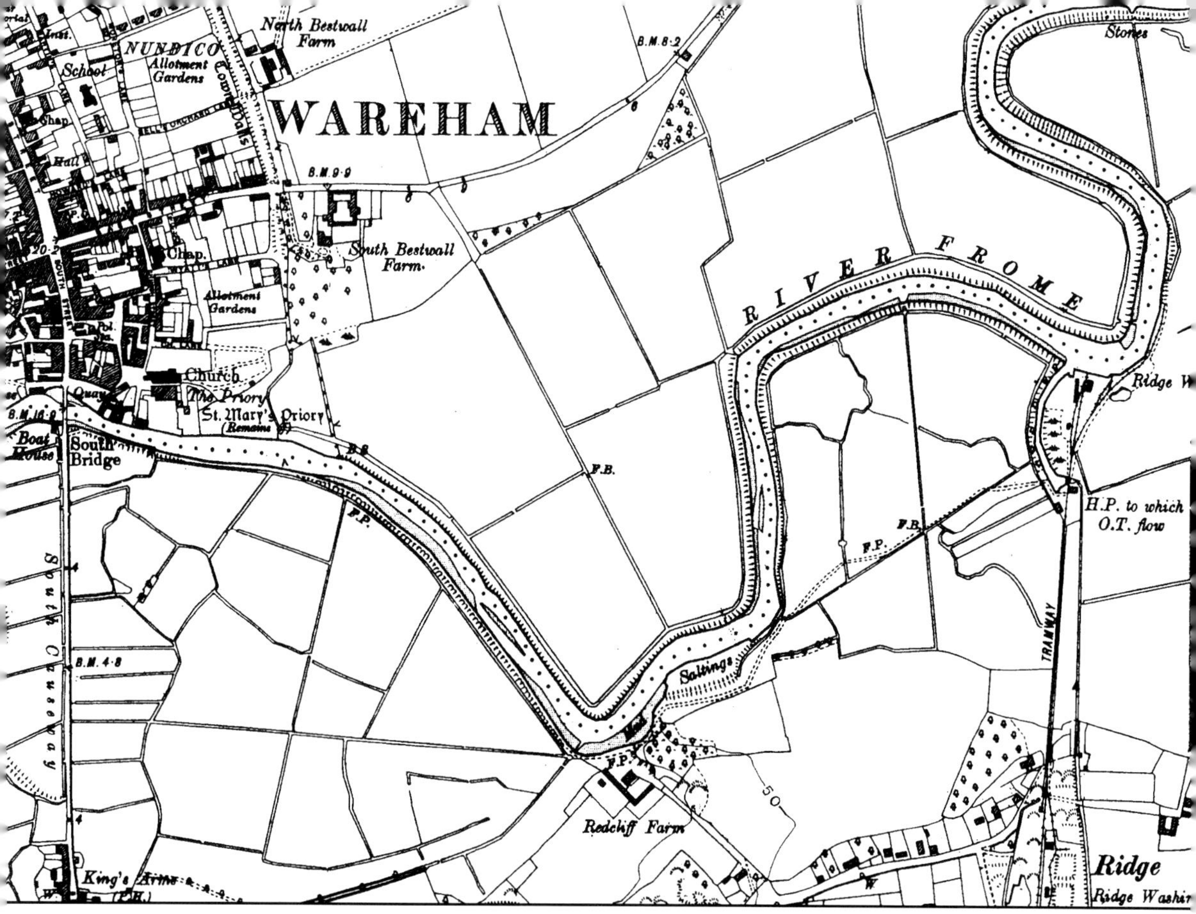

The line top right on the previous map continued to Ridge Wharf, which opened in 1838 and was two miles from Furzebrook. This section was not used after 1940 and all narrow gauge operation at Furzebrook had ceased by 1957. The drying shed (lower right) became a listed structure in 1998.

1.25   Latin names were used for the entire steam locomotive fleet of seven. *Sextus* was built by Peckett in 1925, photographed in 1950 and withdrawn in 1956. *Primus* was an 0-4-2T from Belliss & Seekings' Birmingham works in 1866. (B.M.Barber/R.M.Casserley coll.)

1.26   *Septimus* is seen in helpful low sunlight in December 1946. Built by Peckett in 1930, it was slightly smaller than *Sextus*. It was purchased for preservation in 1955, but scrapped in 1962. (J.K.Williams coll.)

1.27   *Secundus* had better luck and a second life in preservation. It was built in 1874, by Belliss & Seekings; the skirts suggest that it was intended for a street tramway. (R.M.Casserley coll.)

1.28   A fine panorama from 30th August 1944 includes both engine sheds, together with *Tertius* (left) and *Quintus*. The former (an 0-6-0ST) came from Manning Wardle in 1886 and lasted until 1959. The latter (an 0-4-0ST) was from the same builder in 1914 and ran until 1956. (L.W.Perkins/F.A.Wycherley coll.)

1.29   A closer view of *Tertius* on the same day reveals its early ancestry. Only the front plate survived from the original cab. It had been built by Manning Wardle as no. 999 in 1886. (L.W.Perkins/F.A.Wycherley coll.)

1.30   This charming masterpiece is from August 1954. The track is worthy of study. The locomotive is *Quintus* and is described in caption 1.33. (Ivo Peters/P.Q.Treloar coll.)

1.31   The rear view of *Secundus* reveals garden shed as well as tram engine features, plus rope and chain to meet all eventualities. It was rebuilt by Stephen Lewin in 1880 and reboilered by Peckett & Sons in 1936. (W.Gilbert/P.Q.Treloar coll.)

1.32   A final shot of *Secundus* shows clearly its marine boiler, a type devoid of a conventional firebox and ash pan. The grate is part way up the extended boiler barrel. The engine went to the Museum of Science & Technology in Birmingham in 1955, having been saved by the Birmingham Locomotive Club. (J.K.Williams coll.)

1.33   *Quintus* was purchased from Manning Wardle new in 1914. It was rebuilt in 1934 and served here until 1956, often hauling these ungainly end tipping wagons. (J.K.Williams coll.)

1.34   We complete our survey of this site with six photographs from 20th January 1956, the last year of full railway operation. Economy of operation was essential; only two brake blocks are visible and they were wooden. (H.C.Casserley)

1.35   Braking on the nearest wagon is by rail sledge, whereas the other is more conventional. The clay is slightly more ball shape after the weathering period. (H.C.Casserley)

1.36   Road transport is intruding and the shed on the right has lost its rail connection. *Tertius* is in the background of a system in terminal decline. The weathering beds were rail-worked into 1957. (H.C.Casserley)

1.37   *Tertius* received the boiler from the engine seen in picture 1.40 in 1951, but its firebox was too wide to fit within the frame. This explains the high boiler pitch, seen to advantage at the exchange sidings. (H.C.Casserley)

1.38   A view east along the main line shows a modest degree of track maintenance for a doomed railway. No comment need be made about the siding on the left. It was all lifted by 1959. (H.C.Casserley)

1.39   The business became part of English China Clays in 1968 and this siding was used until 1982 and again between 1986 and 1992. The nearby Furzebrook gas terminal siding closed in March 2005 and thus industrial railways on the Isle of Purbeck came to an end. (H.C.Casserley)

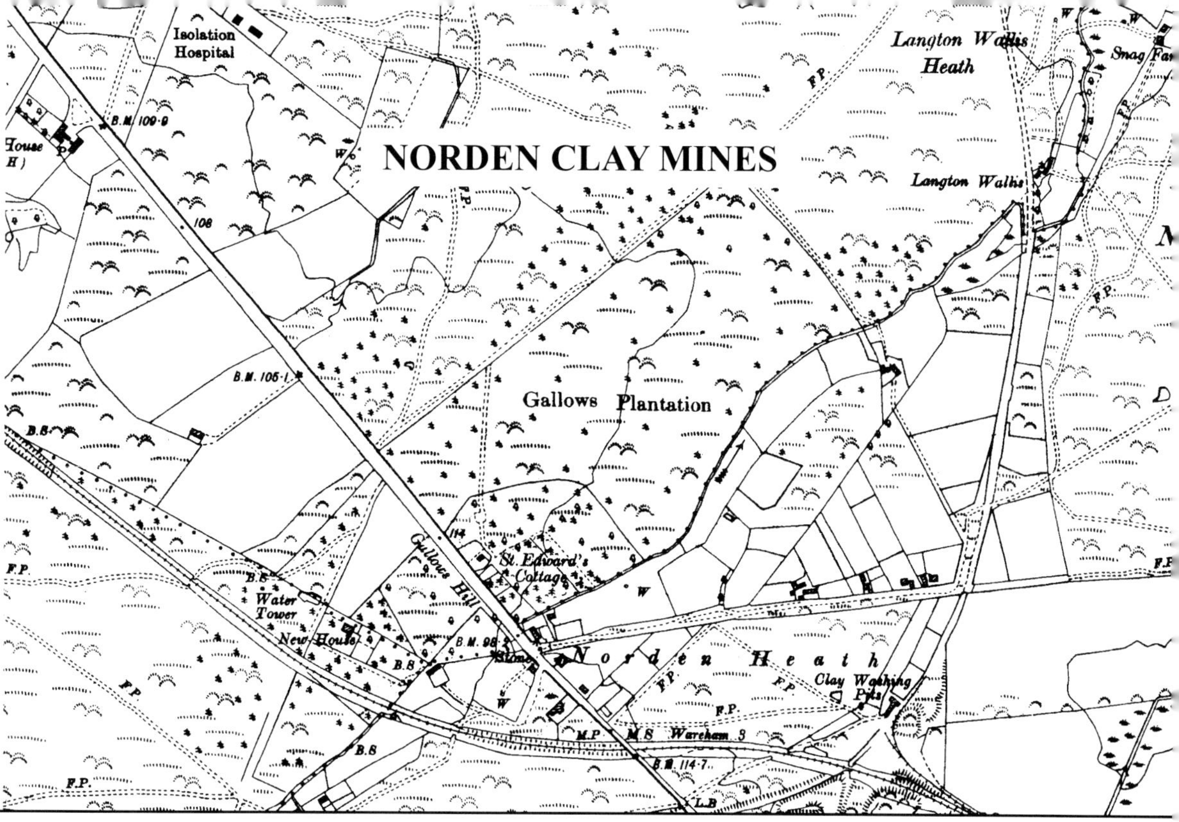

NORDEN CLAY MINES

Gallows Plantation

Langton Wallis Heath

Langton Wallis

Gallows Hill

St. Edward's Cottage

Water Tower

New House

Norden Heath

Clay Washing Pits

M.P. M.S. Wareham 9

This 6ins to 1 mile map continues on the next page to Norden Works. The lane to Langton Wallis was the route of the tramway to Middlebere Quay. All the tramways on these maps were known as Fayle's Tramway and were 3ft 9ins gauge.

1.40   One of Fayle's Tramway's two steam locomotives was this 0-4-0T built by Stephen Lewin in Poole in 1868. It was for long named *Tiny* and was in use until 1948. The photograph is from 1933. (H.F.Wheeller/P.Q.Treloar coll.)

The terminus at Middlebere Quay is shown on the 1901 edition at 25ins to 1 mile. The line closed in about 1907.

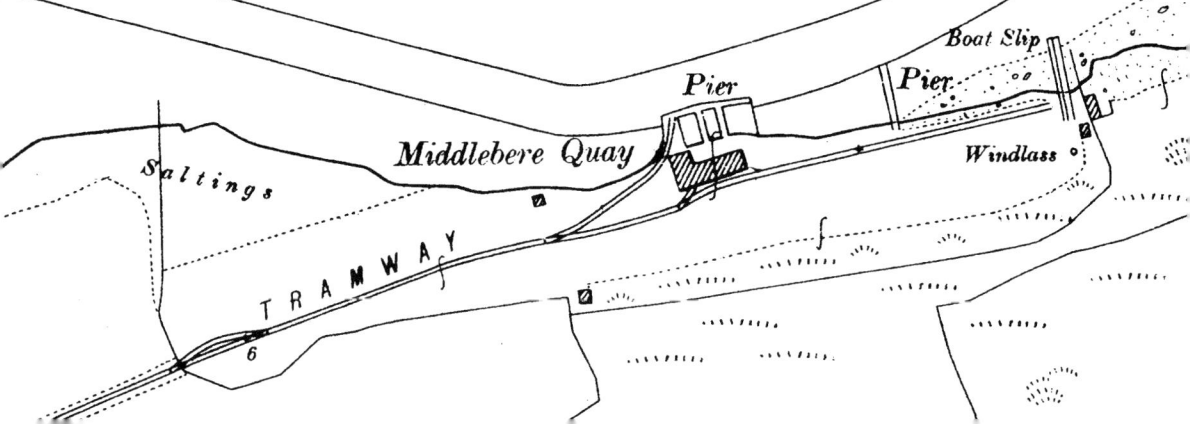

Boat Slip

Pier

Pier

Middlebere Quay

Windlass

Saltings

TRAMWAY

6

1.41   The other regular performer was the 0-4-0ST *Thames*, a Manning Wardle product of 1902, which was purchased in 1909 from the contractors for the Barking sewage outfall works of the LCC. It is seen in 1932, having been rebuilt from 3ft 6ins gauge. It was scrapped in 1948. Northeast of Norden was a line to Goathorn Pier, known as the Newton Tramway. (P.Q.Treloar coll.)

The maps are from 1900.

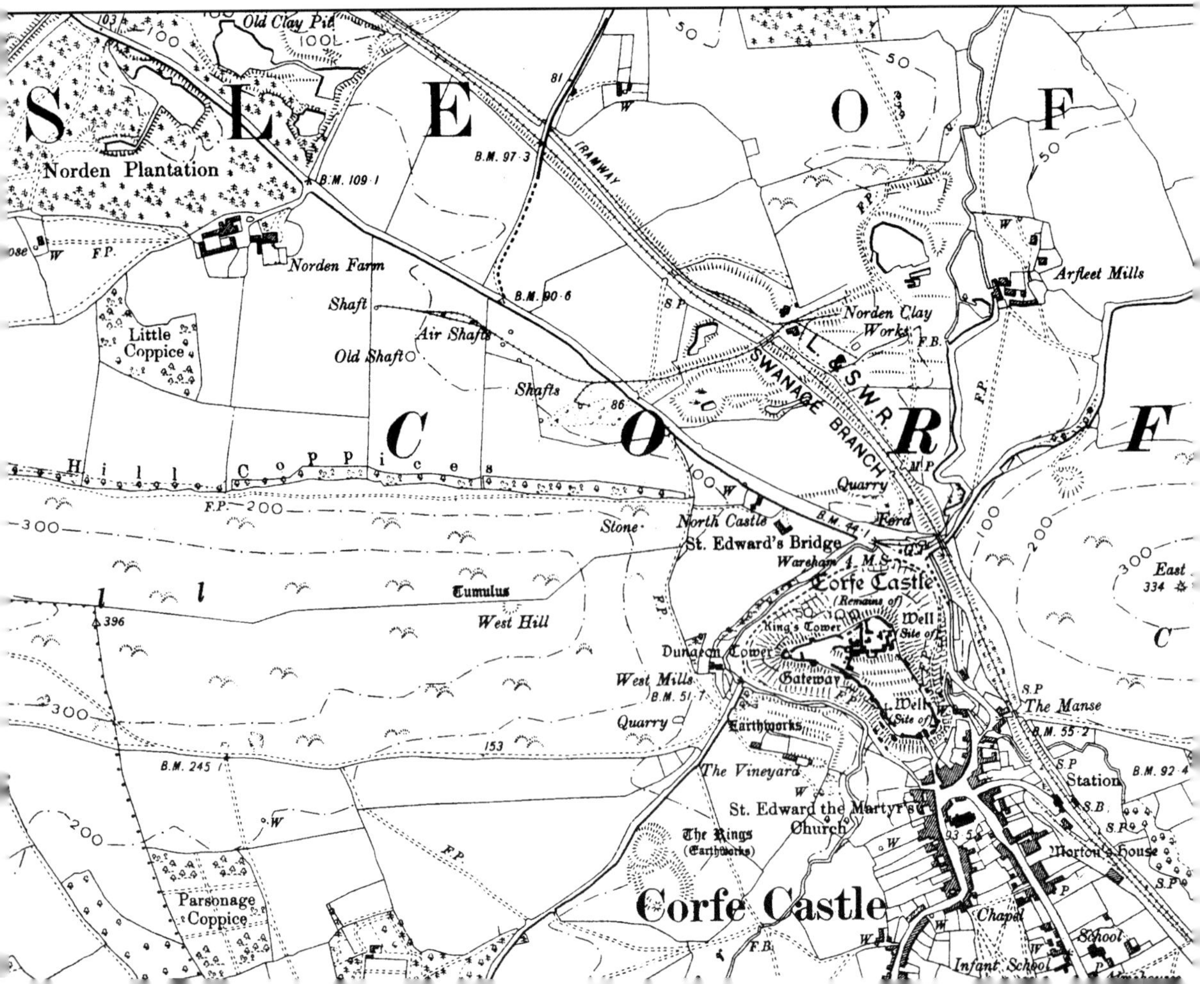

1.42   After the closure of the school at Goathorn, about ten children of clay workers were conveyed to and from Corfe Castle in this mobile shed, hauled by *Thames*. The council paid for this service for several years in the 1930s. (S.P.W.Corbett)

1.43   The long line to Goathorn Pier was closed in about 1939 and the remaining sections were relaid to "two-foot" gauge (1ft 11½ ins) in 1948. This is a 1936 Orenstein & Koppel diesel, at work on 10th April 1950. (J.H.Meredith)

1.44   The works was recorded on the same day; at least the track was in good condition, if not the buildings. (J.H.Meredith)

1.45   Five photographs from 1952 follow. One steam and three other locomotives were purchased at the time of the regauging. This is a petrol engined Motor Rail, with a misleading radiator. (S.W.Baker)

1.46　　The china clay deposits are 30 to 50ft thick and were dug manually. The skip wagons were rope hauled out of the pit. (S.W.Baker)

1.47　　A pneumatically operated spade is being used by the man on the left, the lumps of clay being known as "balls". These were taken away and tipped to weather for several months before processing. (S.W.Baker)

1.48   Ruston & Hornsby no. 179889 of 1936 is pushing its train onto the weighbridge, which is below the second wagon from the far end. Rushes grow in the track, indicating its waterlogged foundation. (S.W.Baker)

1.49   *Russell* was built in 1906 by Hunslet for the Portmadoc, Beddgelert & South Snowdon Railway, which was never completed. However, it did run over this route when the Welsh Highland Railway constructed the line. (S.W.Baker)

1.50   After the WHR came under the control of the Festiniog Railway, the cab was subjected to unsuccessful surgery. The loco eventually hauled ironstone at Hook Norton in Oxfordshire during World War II. It was purchased as a 2-6-2T in 1948, but problems with its leading axle were solved by simply removing it. It moved clay until 1953 and was saved from the scrapmen by the Birmingham Locomotive Club. It is seen out of use in April 1955, before moving to the museum at Towyn. A further convoluted story has ended with it working again on part of the WHR. (W.Vaughan-Jenkins/ P.Q.Treloar coll.)

1.51   Further withdrawn locos were recorded on 28th July 1964. Nearest is Orenstein & Koppel no. 21160 and behind is Motor Rail no. 5252. (C.G.Down)

1.52   Five more photographs from the same day follow. Ruston no. 175413 of 1936 is with a train at the rail-road tip. (C.G.Down)

1.53 A general view near the workshops reveals the basic nature of the engineering practised, with running rails forming a lifting gantry. Was it certified, one wonders? (C.G.Down)

1.54 Much of the equipment was then life expired and standing near the workshops. Evident here is the road-rail loading facility. (C.G.Down)

1.55 Ruston no. 392117 of 1956 is propelling a train near the workshops. (C.G.Down)

1.56   The main line is on the right, while on the left is the branch to the underground mine loading plant. (C.G.Down)

1.57   Three pictures from 29th August 1968 include some interesting details. Bogie wagons stand near the rail-road transfer depot, loaded with gorse. (C.G.Maggs)

1.58   The level crossing over the A351 was protected by a catch point. Modern Mad Motorists could do with such a facility in the road, to protect rail users. (C.G.Maggs)

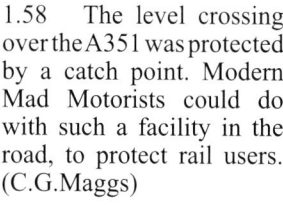

1.59   The bridge over the Swanage branch was unusual in its design. Fortunately it still stands and can be seen in side view in picture no. 3.11. (C.G.Maggs)

1.60   The clay mine is on the left in this panorama of the Purbeck Hills from 9th March 1969. Narrow gauge railway operation ceased in 1972. (M.A.N.Johnston)

1.61 The pithead was recorded on the same day, the shaft being lower left. The controller is above centre. The digging of clay underground ceased in 1998. (M.A.N.Johnston)

Other views of this area can be found in *Wareham to Swanage - 50 years of change.* (Middleton Press)

1.62 The exchange siding was known as Eldon's siding, as Lord Eldon was the landowner. British Railways renamed it Norden Siding in 1950 and it was in use until March 1966. This 1963 view is from the east; the siding entered the shed on the left from the west. (M.A.N.Johnston)

SOUTHERN GAS BOARD
POOLE GASWORKS

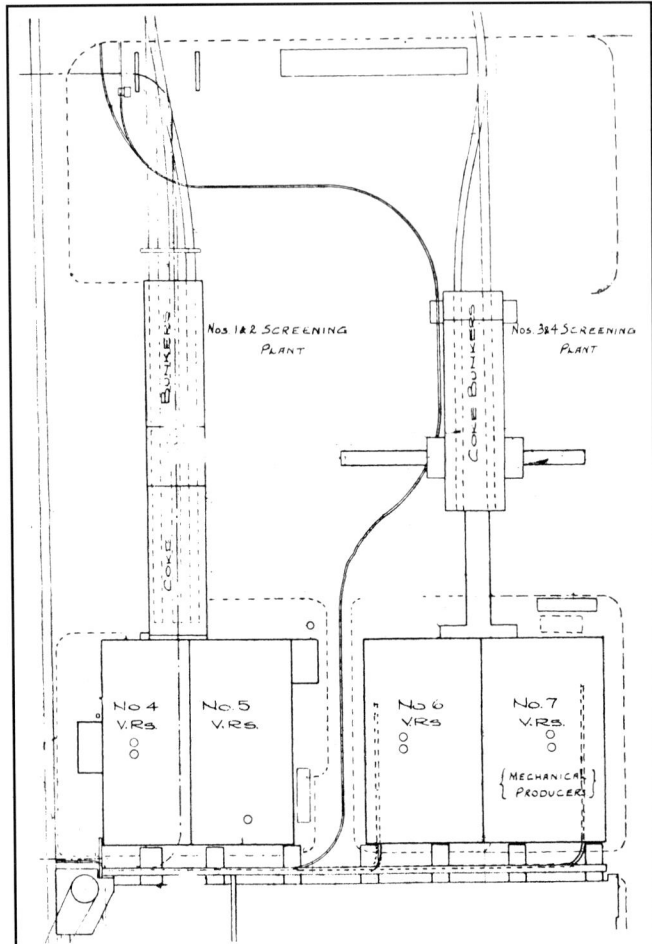

1.L   Rapid increase in demand soon outgrew Poole works and a nearby and much larger site was created by filling-in the tidal creek immediately south of the L&SWR embankment, east of Poole Station. Pitwines Gasworks was built from the early 1920s. It had standard gauge sidings, but coal was still landed at Poole. An aerial ropeway connected the two works; at one point it crossed a public road on a reinforced-concrete bridge. A row of vertical retort houses was built at Pitwines over the years. Much of the internal transport was done by a telpher system, its main task being to carry coke from the retort houses to the coke water gas plant in box-like skips, and to deal with ash. No. 4 retort house of 1922 and No. 5 house of 1930 were served thus. As the number of retort houses grew, it was found inconvenient to extend the telpher track since too many sets of points would have been involved, always a weak point with monorails. At the surprisingly late date of 1944 a two-foot gauge railway was installed to remove ashes from the new No. 6 retort house. In 1950 yet another retort house, No. 7, was added to the row. This time new bunkers and screens were built for the extra coke, but there remained a need to transport a small share of this coke to some point within reach of the telphers, and the ashes also needed to be removed. Ashes were valuable: they were taken to a Pan-ash plant where useful fuel was extracted. The residue went for making building blocks. A second two-foot line was laid out, snaking across the yard on fully-paved track from the new coke bunkers, where the skips were filled from lorry chutes, to a point below the telpher track. A rail weighbridge was purchased from Averys and installed in 1951 near the telpher pick-up. At the same time the original system was extended into the new No. 7 house to receive its ashes. The tracks did not enter the older houses, as they now did with 6 and 7. A connecting track was laid in the gap between 5 and 6 to join the old and new systems together. A spur line was laid to gain access to coke from the original screening plant, the narrow gauge being placed in the centre of the standard gauge siding (not shown on the diagram). Retort houses 6 and especially 7 were the more efficient, so they were the last to close in 1968 when carbonising at Pitwines gave way to naphtha reforming. Gas was last made at Pitwines in February 1972 and the site has since been completely redeveloped. VR is vertical retort.

1.63 Two photographs from 20th October 1967 show one of the two Lister diesels. Both were preserved, after being bought by Alan Keef Ltd in 1968 and 1970. (P.Nicholson)

1.64 This features one of the coke hoppers and shows the operating mechanism for the doors. Lister no. 18557 of 1942 was on the location seen in picture no. 3.15 in 2005. (P.Nicholson)

SWANAGE PIER RAILWAY

The stone-built pier was completed in 1858 and it had a tramway of standard gauge. It later became 2ft 6ins gauge. The 1886 map shows the stone yards or bankers along the sea front. Soon after the branch opened in 1884, they were moved inland, near the station.

1.65   The steamer pier was added in 1896 and was also used by fishing vessels. The tramway was used to convey coal to them. (D.Haysom coll.)

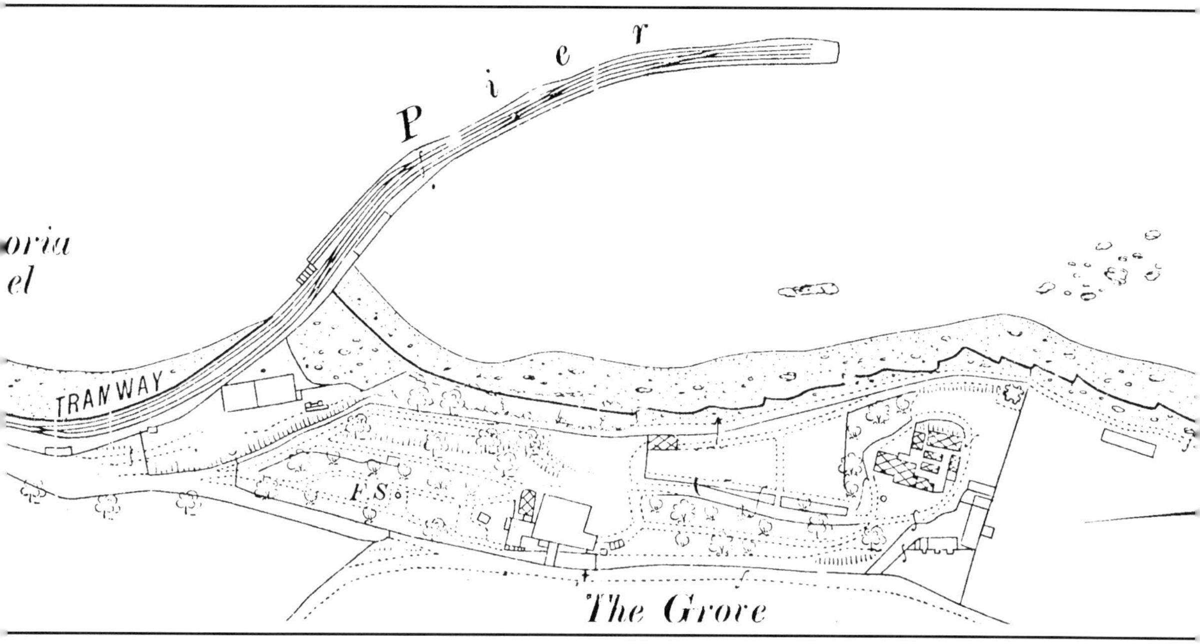

_P   i   e   r_

oria
_el_

TRANWAY

F.S.

The Grove

1.66   Much manual effort was required to load and unload the coal wagons, which are seen in about 1910. The original plan had been to take the tramway inland to the quarries. (J.Ward coll.)

1.67   Swanage was transformed into a holiday resort and the stone industry was moved to the back of the town. This panorama is from around 1900. (D.Haysom coll.)

1.68   Sections of tramway were still visible in 1968, although it had last been used in the 1930s, albeit in a limited way. This is where the road crossed to a slipway. (D.Cullum)

1.69   The track at the shore end had been encased in concrete for many decades, but this was removed in 1994. The building on the right had served variously as a fish warehouse, a coal store and sometimes as a temporary mortuary. (V.Mitchell)

1.70   A link with a past era was made on 3rd September 1995, when the *PS Waverley* called at Swanage. The old coaling pier was in poor condition by that time, but served as a reminder of an unfulfilled tramway project. (P.G.Barnes)

VICKERS ENGINEERING
WYKE REGIS

1.71   Wyke Regis is at the north end of the causeway leading to Portland and the pier is on the east side of it, in sheltered water further protected by extensive harbour arms, seen in both of these 1967 photographs. (P.Nicholson)

1.72   The Whitehead Engineering premises had been subject to high security as they had been used in connection with the production of torpedoes and the two-foot gauge tramway carried these to the ships. It had a battery-electric trolley, built in 1929. The pier was dismantled in 1968. The nearby halt is illustrated in our *Branch Lines around Weymouth*. (P.Nicholson)

The 1929 survey at 25ins to 1 mile shows the line from the works to the pier passing under the single line Portland branch and a parallel siding. The torpedo had been invented in the 1860s and the factory was begun here in 1891. Vickers-Armstrong became involved in 1928 and gears were the main product by 1958. Pistons and other items were manufactured from 1966 until the works closed in 1994.

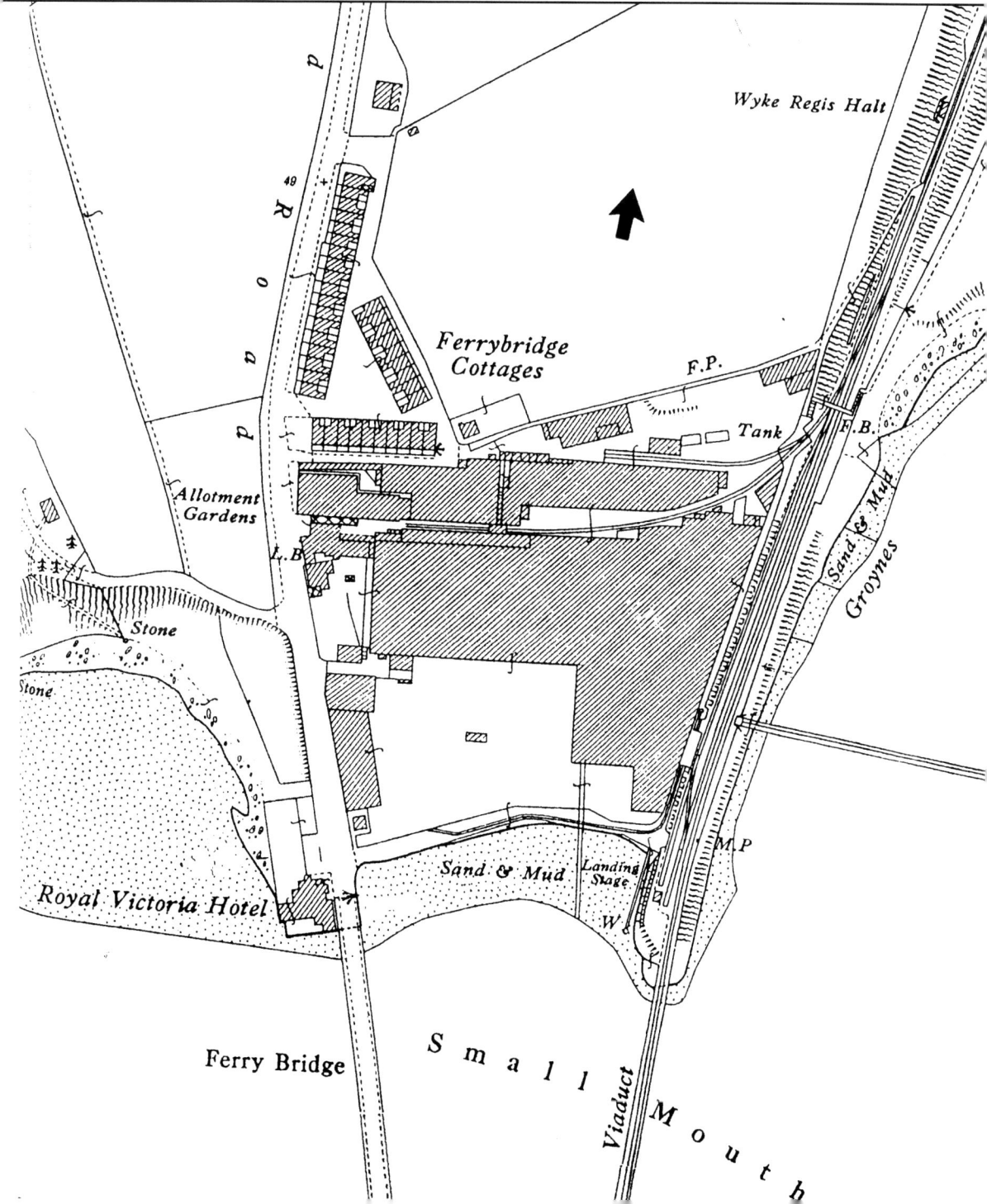

WEYMOUTH & PORTLAND
LONG SEA OUTFALL

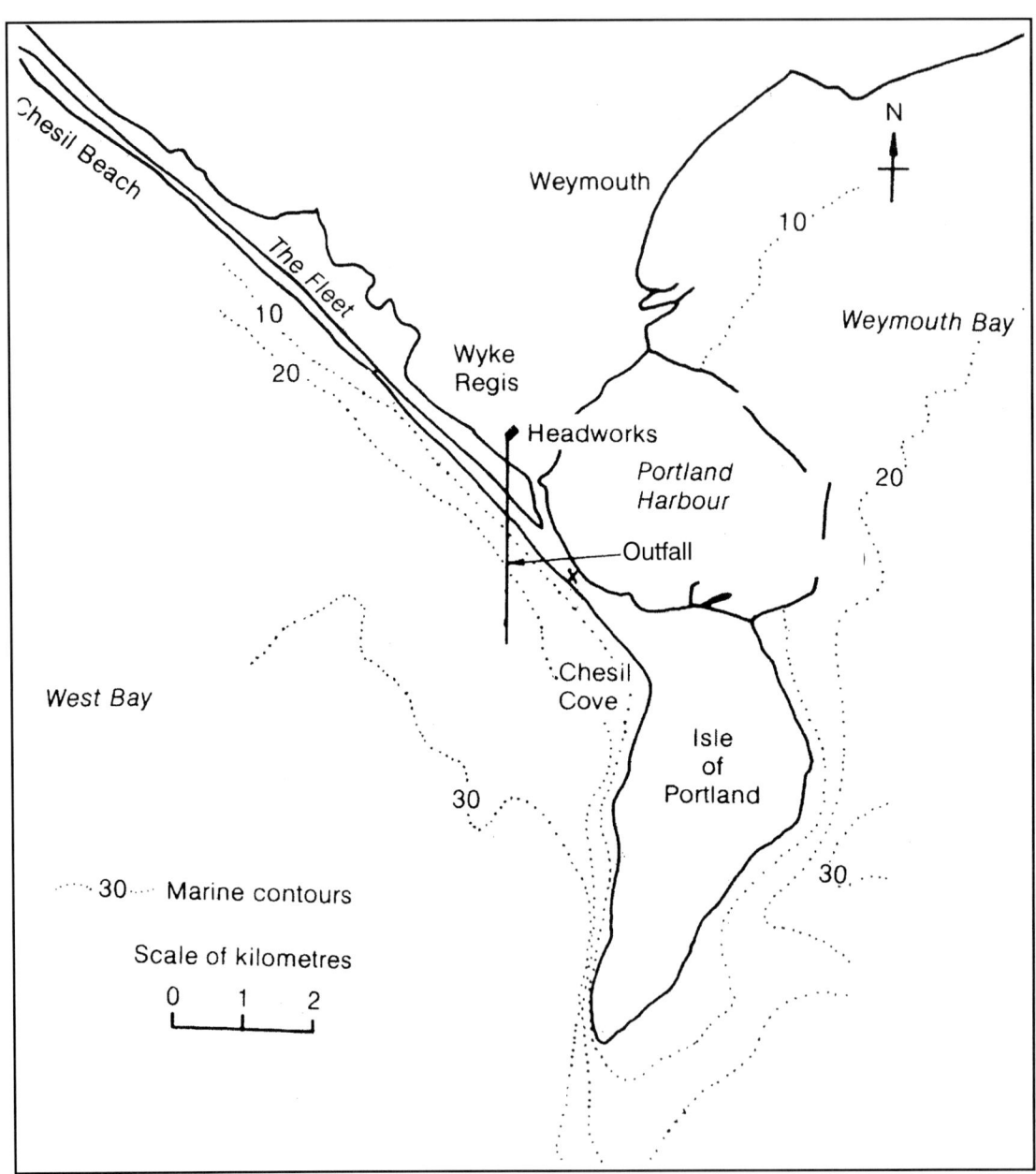

In July 1983 Edmund Nuttall Ltd completed the Outfall Tunnel. Measuring 1.67m in diameter the tunnel carries treated effluent from a headworks building, situated on the cliff top at Wyke Regis, to a sea bed diffuser point 2.8km offshore in West Bay.

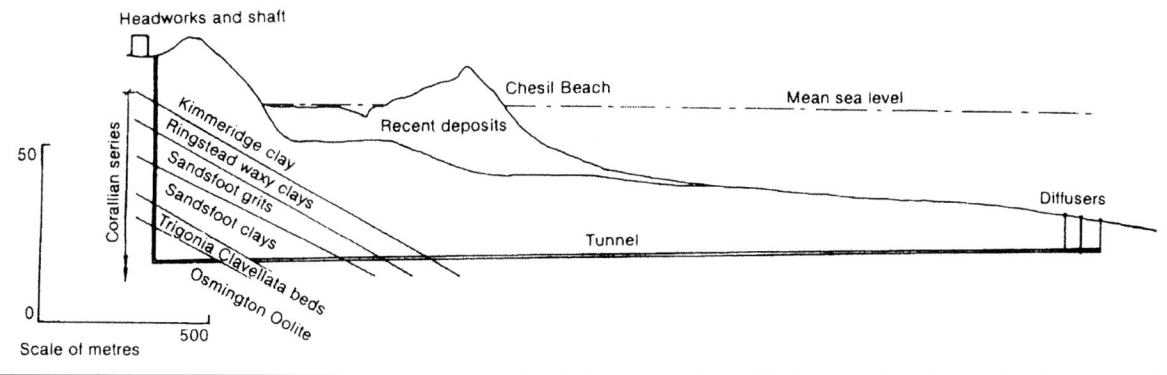

Longitudinal sections show the shaft and tunnel, together with the geology.

1.73 The 1.60m diameter tunnel was driven from a 40m long, 3.2m diameter twin track marshalling tunnel constructed at the base of the 60m deep access shaft. Purpose designed 2ft gauge, 30 lb.yd trackwork and rolling stock were used to transport men, lining segments, materials and excavated spoil. To minimise headroom, the rails were clipped to curved sleepers laid directly on the tunnel invert and 1.3m³ capacity steel body skips were carried inside low headroom chassis. The battery box on each 4 tonne, 16hp Clayton locomotive was removed and transported behind the locomotive on a separate wagon. An equivalent weight of ballast concrete was placed on each locomotive chassis and the driver, together with his control unit, repositioned inside a low cab for safety. A strategically positioned enlargement was constructed to allow trains to pass.
(Edmund Nuttall Ltd)

ROYAL NAVAL CORDITE FACTORY HOLTON HEATH

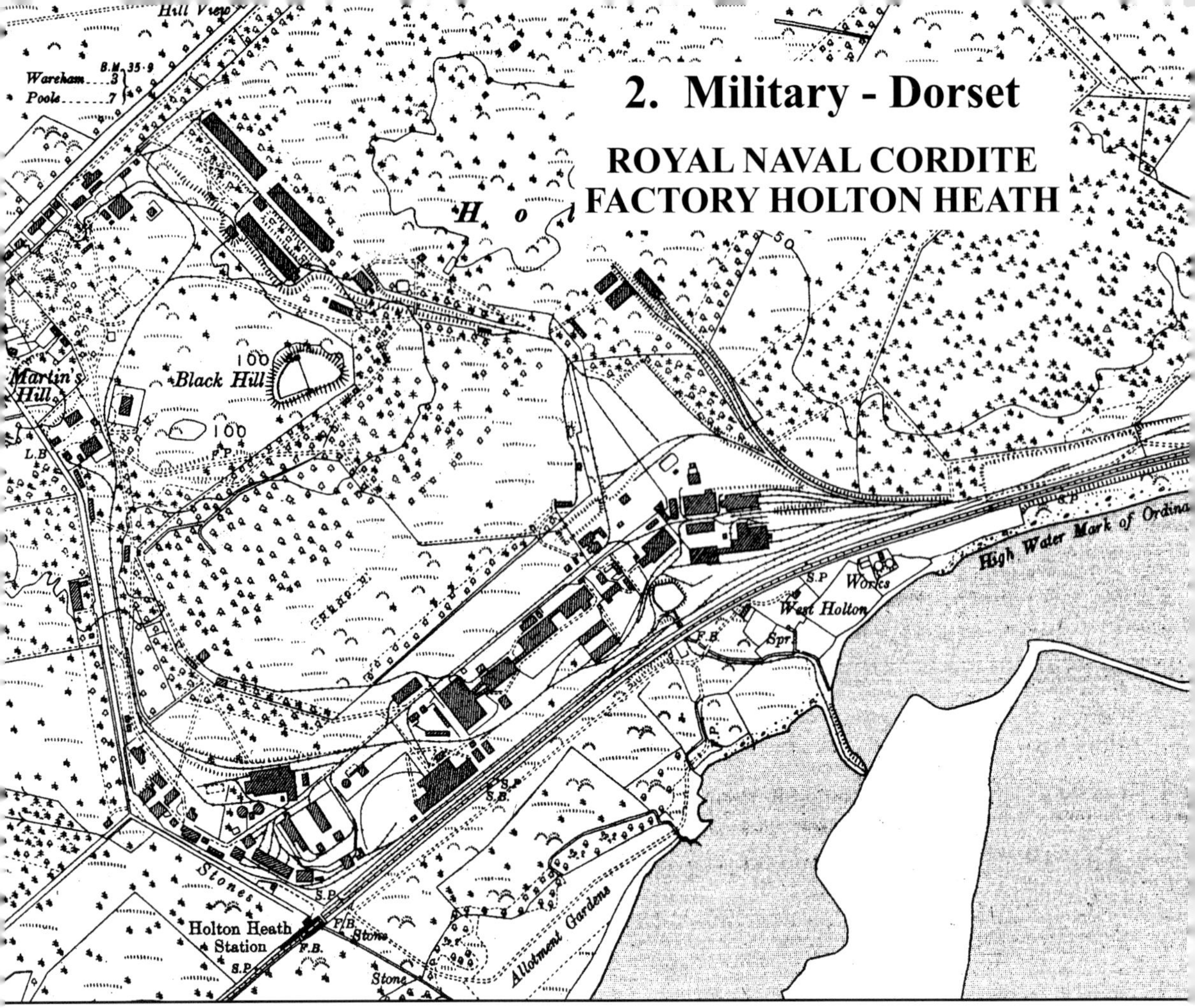

Hill View

B.M. 35·9
Wareham 3
Poole 7

H o

Martin's
Hill

Black Hill
100
100
P.P.

L.B.

High Water Mark of Ordina

S.P. Works
West Holton
P.B. Spr

Stones

Holton Heath
Station
P.B.
Stone
Stone

S.B.

Allotment Gardens

← ——— The factory was built in 1914-15, at the insistence of the First Lord of the Admiralty, Winston Churchill. The Navy needed its own source of propellants, which were made mainly from nitroglycerine and gun cotton. A site remote from habitation was chosen, owing to the explosion risk. One did take place at the factory in June 1931, killing ten workers. This extract from the 6ins to 1 mile survey of 1925 is about five miles west of Poole. One of the standard gauge tracks above the main line on the right continued to Rocklea Jetty, where cordite was loaded onto barges. It passed over the mainline, the bridge abutments still being visible in 2006. Trains for shift workers ran three times a day between Wareham and Christchurch for many years.

← ——— 2.1   The extent of the 2ft 6ins gauge railway was eventually about 14 miles. This section was photographed in about 1915 and the route is now used by the road between the A351 and Holton Heath Industrial Estate.

2.2   Cordite is in transit to the press house on a battery electric vehicle with spark-proof equipment. Even the overalls had tapes instead of metal buttons to emphasise the safety issue. Nitroglycerine was conveyed on waggonways - rubber wheels running in asphalt grooves and hand propelled.

2.3   Battery electric locomotives were also employed; 34 narrow gauge locomotives of different types were recorded, plus three of standard gauge. Press House P10 is in the background, but none of the 27,500 trees planted in 1927 to form camouflage are visible. No damage was caused by bombing, owing to the success of two decoy sites. The one nearby at Arne received 206 bombs in one night alone.

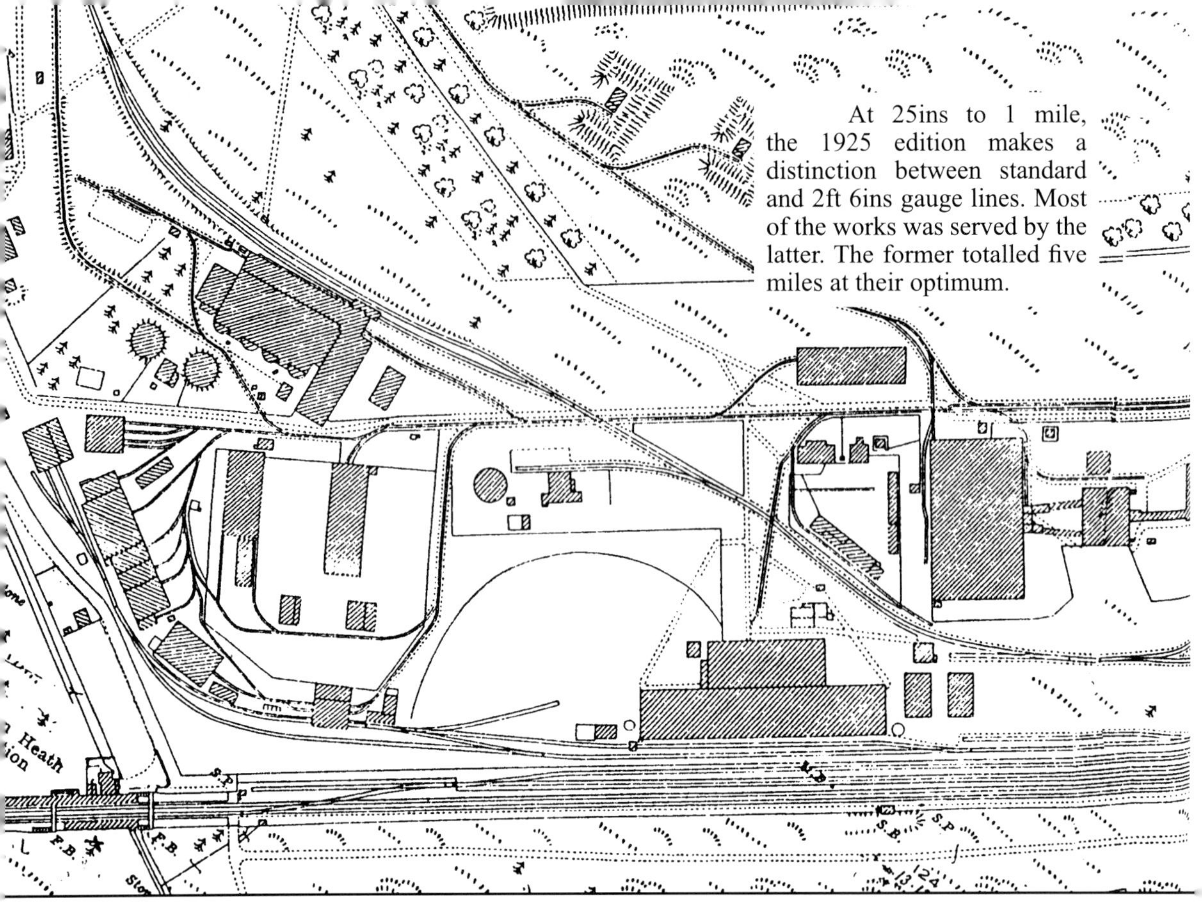

At 25ins to 1 mile, the 1925 edition makes a distinction between standard and 2ft 6ins gauge lines. Most of the works was served by the latter. The former totalled five miles at their optimum.

2.4   Picrite is the component essential for the production of flashless cordite. The lack of flash reduced gun barrel wear, but the main purpose of flashless cordite was to avoid showing presence to the enemy. If the flash could not be seen, return fire would be less effective. Surrounded by blast containing banks is Picrite Drying Stove N11; the wagons are having hot air ducted into them. Most of the final product was taken by barge to Priddy's Hard, Gosport, or Upnor Castle, near Rochester.

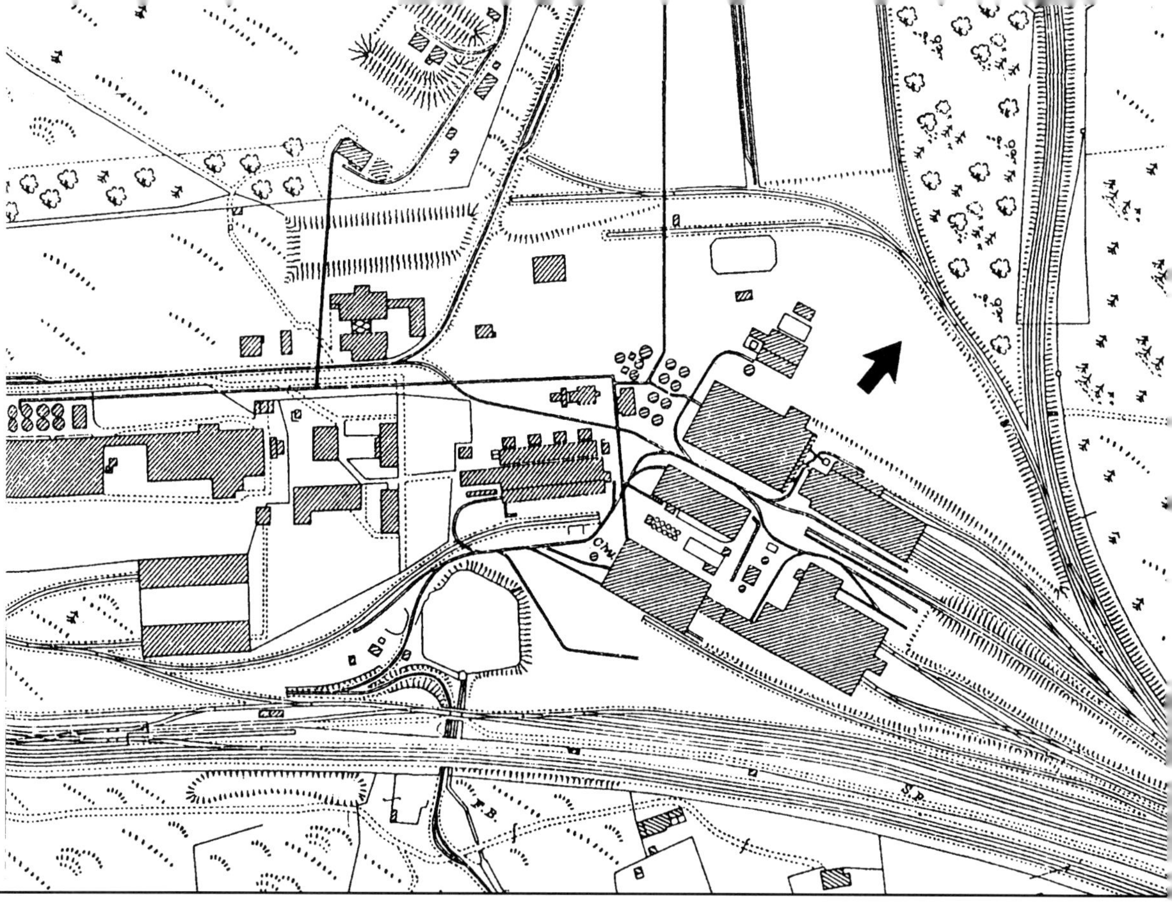

2.5 This fireless locomotive was built by Andrew Barclay in 1916 for this factory, which supplied steam from its power station boilers for the engine. Propellant production ceased here in 1946 and all Naval requirements were provided from Caerwent thereafter. However, some rocket propellant received final processing at Holton Heath subsequently. Part of the site was sold in 1962, mainly for industrial purposes. Some of the plans that follow can be positioned by reference to the six-inch scale map, but they are of a later date. The chemistry is outside the scope of this volume, but we should explain that NG refers to nitroglycerine and not narrow gauge. We apologise for some words having been cut on the original reproductions. Consent has kindly been given to reproduce these and the photographs from *A Pictorial Record of the Royal Naval Cordite Factory, Holton Heath* by M.R.Bowditch and L.Hayward.

Northwest area

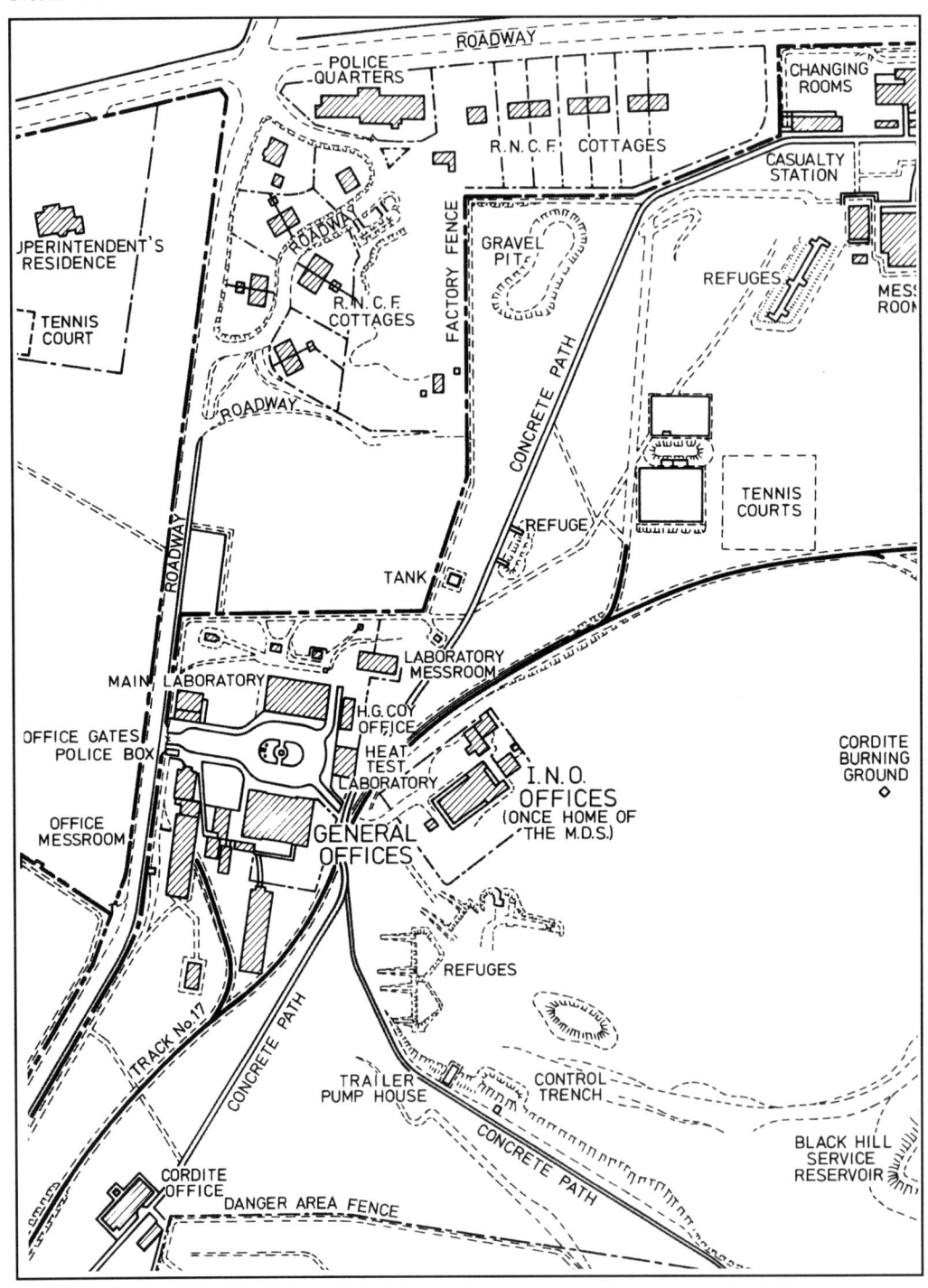

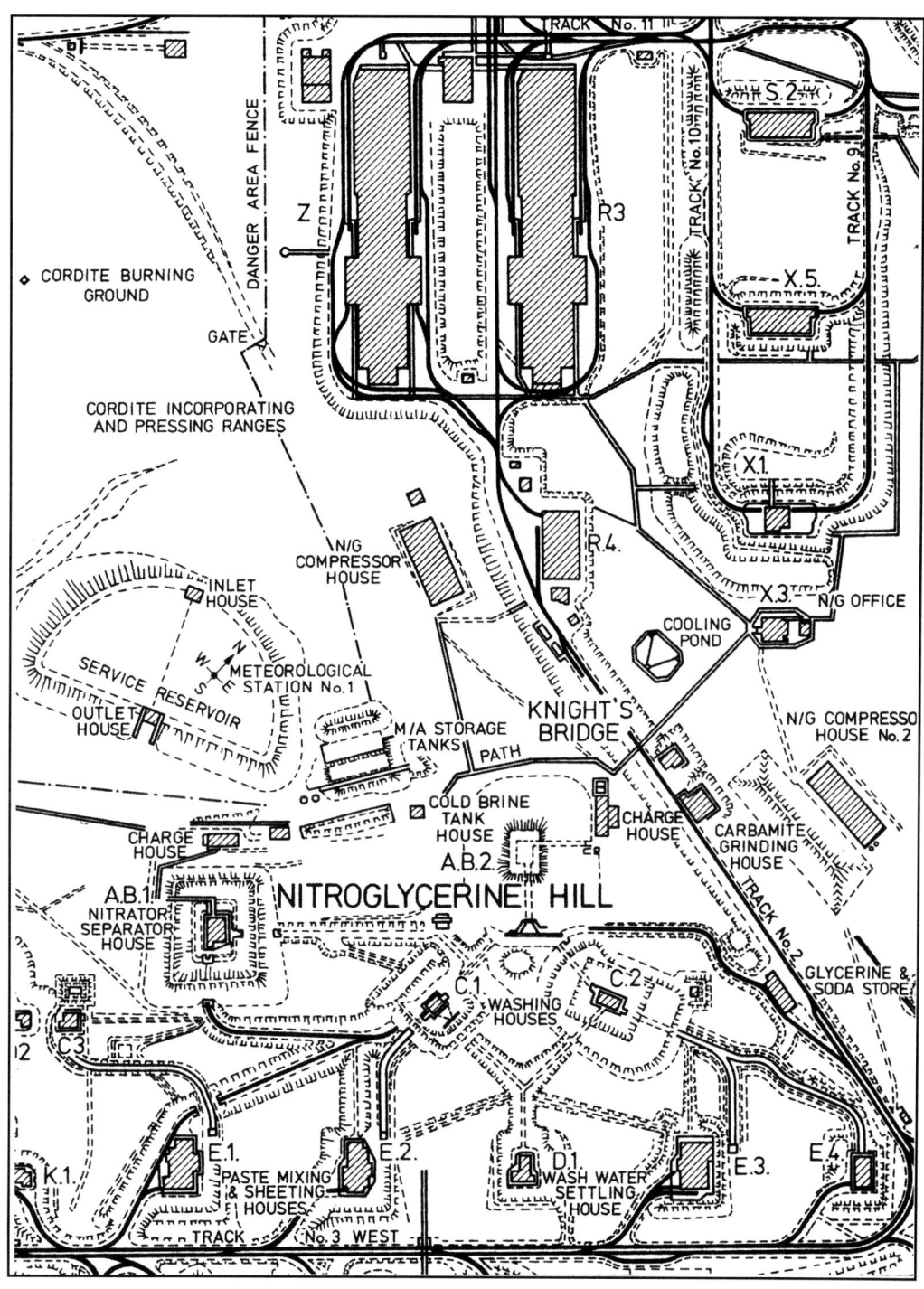

CORDITE BURNING GROUND

DANGER AREA FENCE

GATE

CORDITE INCORPORATING AND PRESSING RANGES

Z

R3

TRACK No. 11

S.2

TRACK No. 10

TRACK No. 9

X.5

X.1

N/G COMPRESSOR HOUSE

R.4.

X.3

N/G OFFICE

COOLING POND

INLET HOUSE

SERVICE RESERVOIR

OUTLET HOUSE

METEOROLOGICAL STATION No.1

M/A STORAGE TANKS

PATH

KNIGHT'S BRIDGE

N/G COMPRESSO HOUSE No. 2

CHARGE HOUSE

COLD BRINE TANK HOUSE

CHARGE HOUSE

CARBAMITE GRINDING HOUSE

A.B.2.

CHARGE HOUSE

A.B.1.

NITRATOR SEPARATOR HOUSE

NITROGLYCERINE HILL

GLYCERINE & SODA STORE

TRACK No. 2

C.1.

C.2.

WASHING HOUSES

C3

K.1.

E.1.

E.2.

D.1.

WASH WATER SETTLING HOUSE

E.3.

E.4

PASTE MIXING & SHEETING HOUSES

TRACK No. 3 WEST

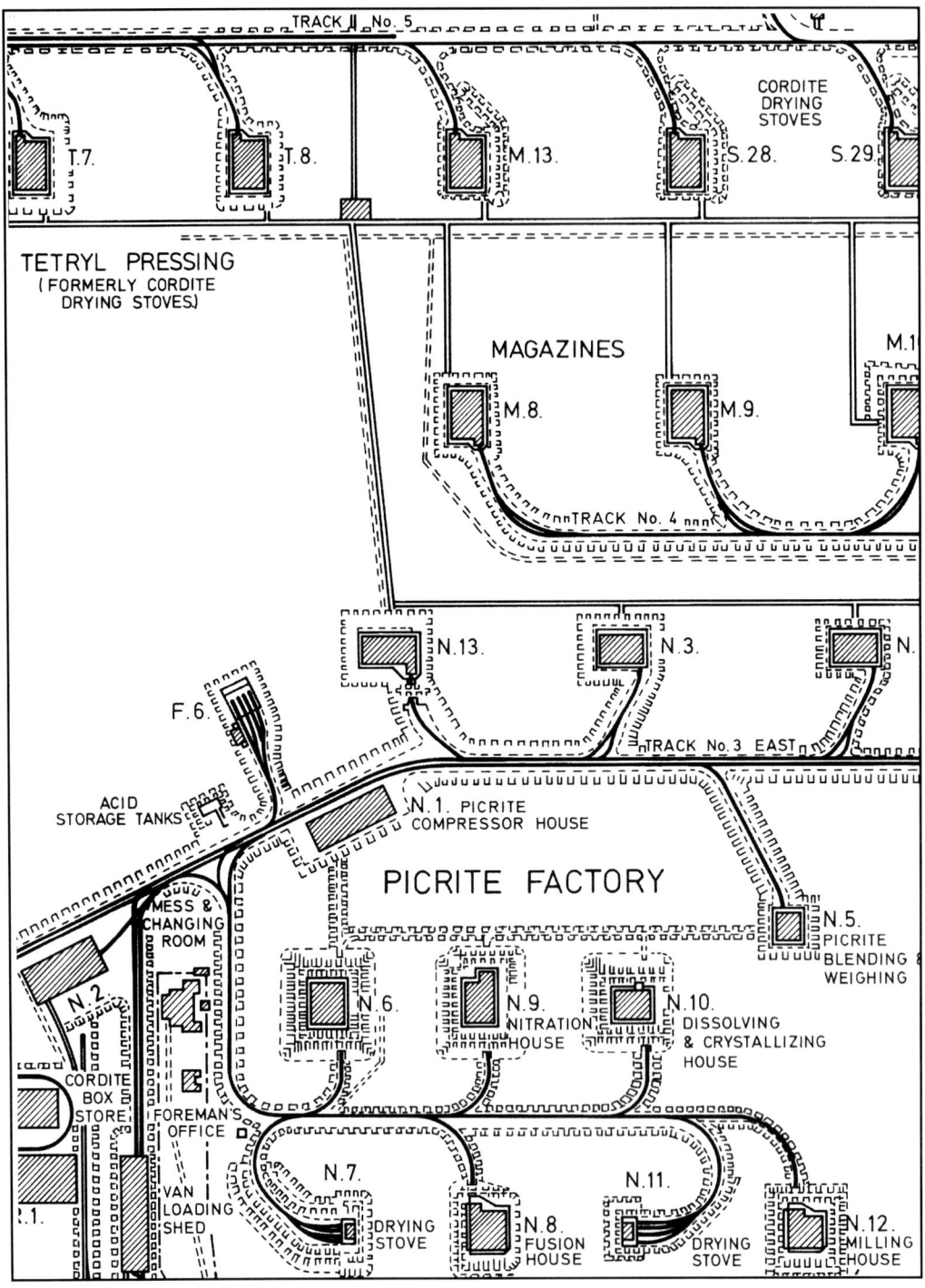

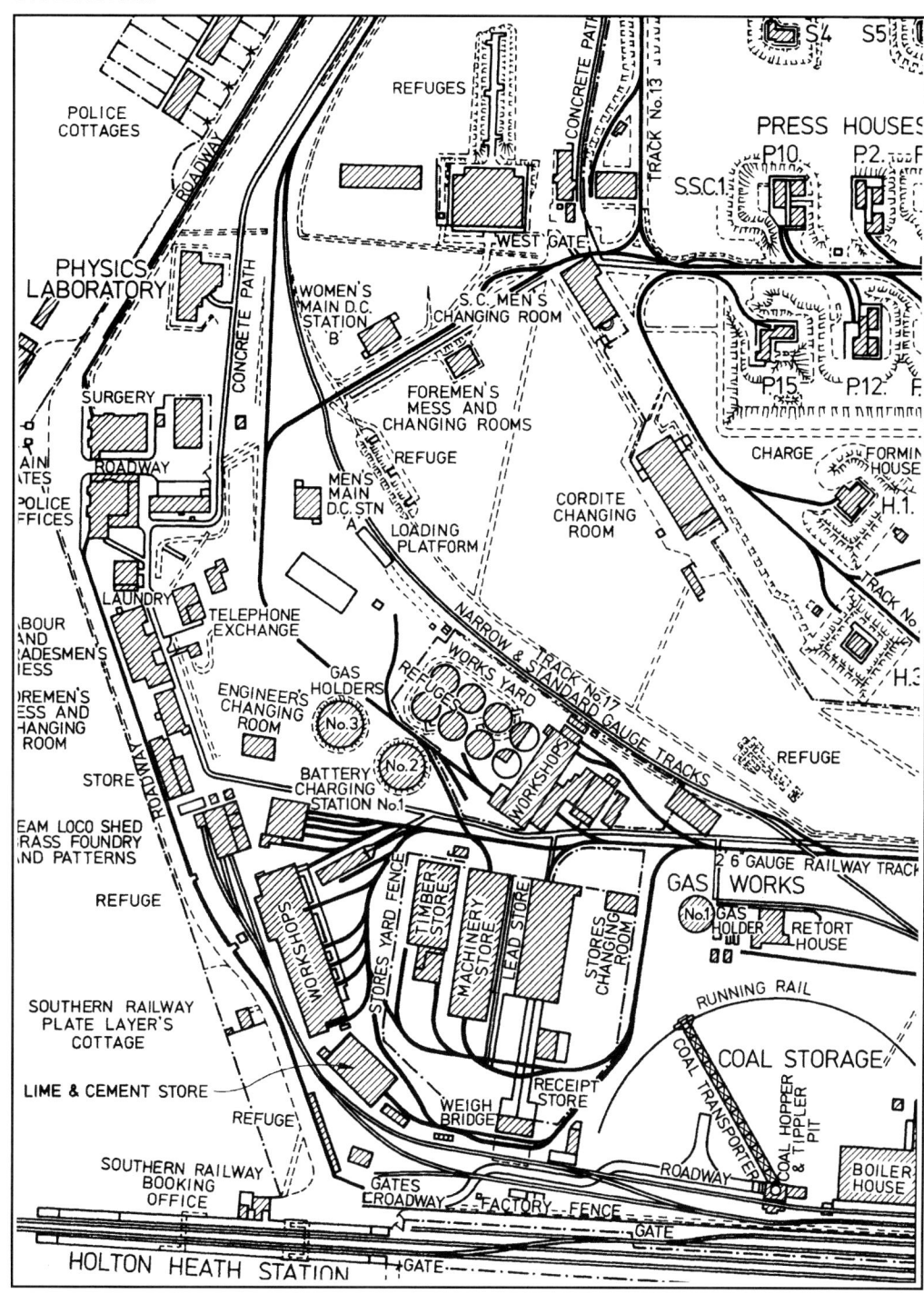

South central area

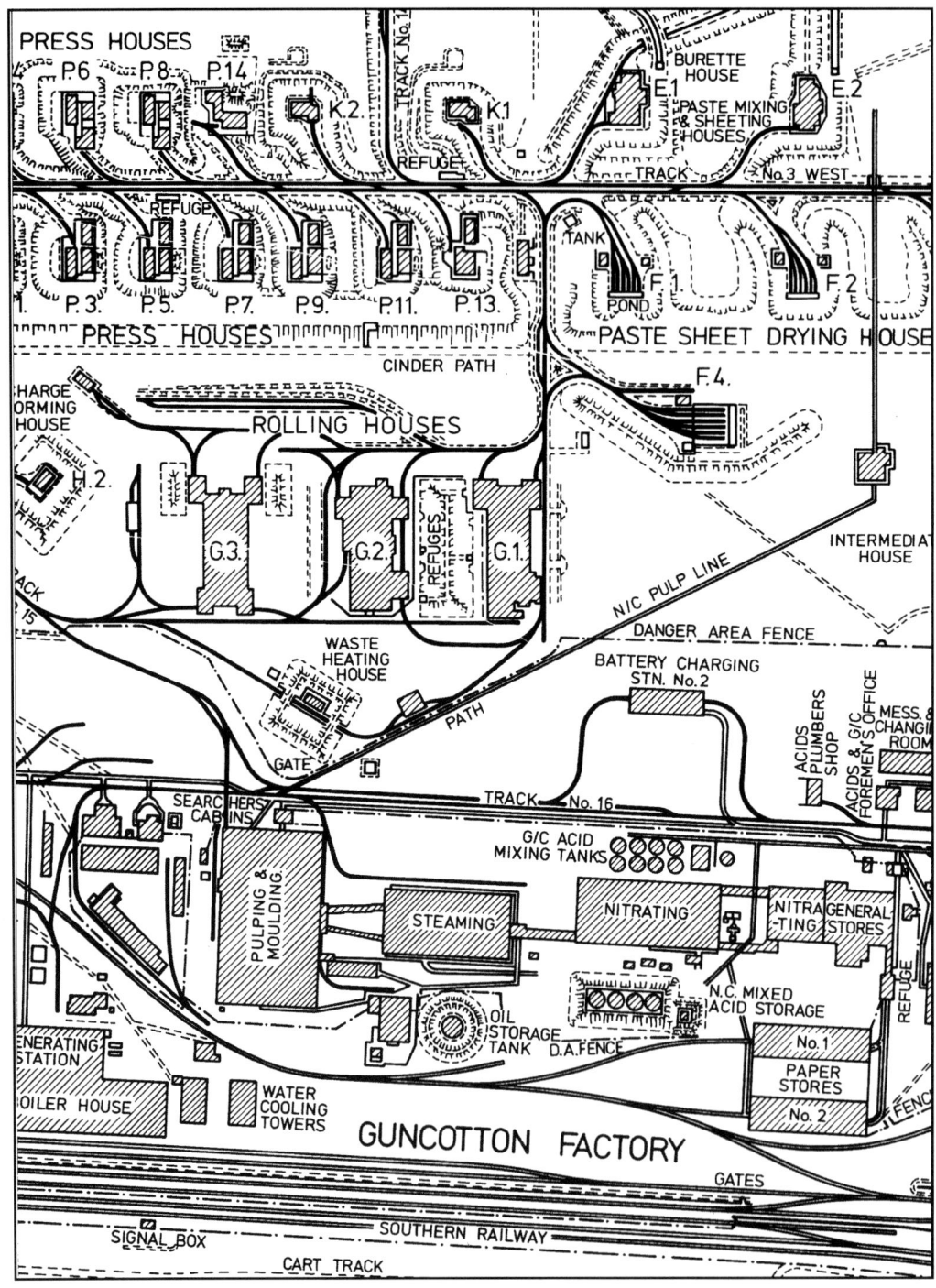

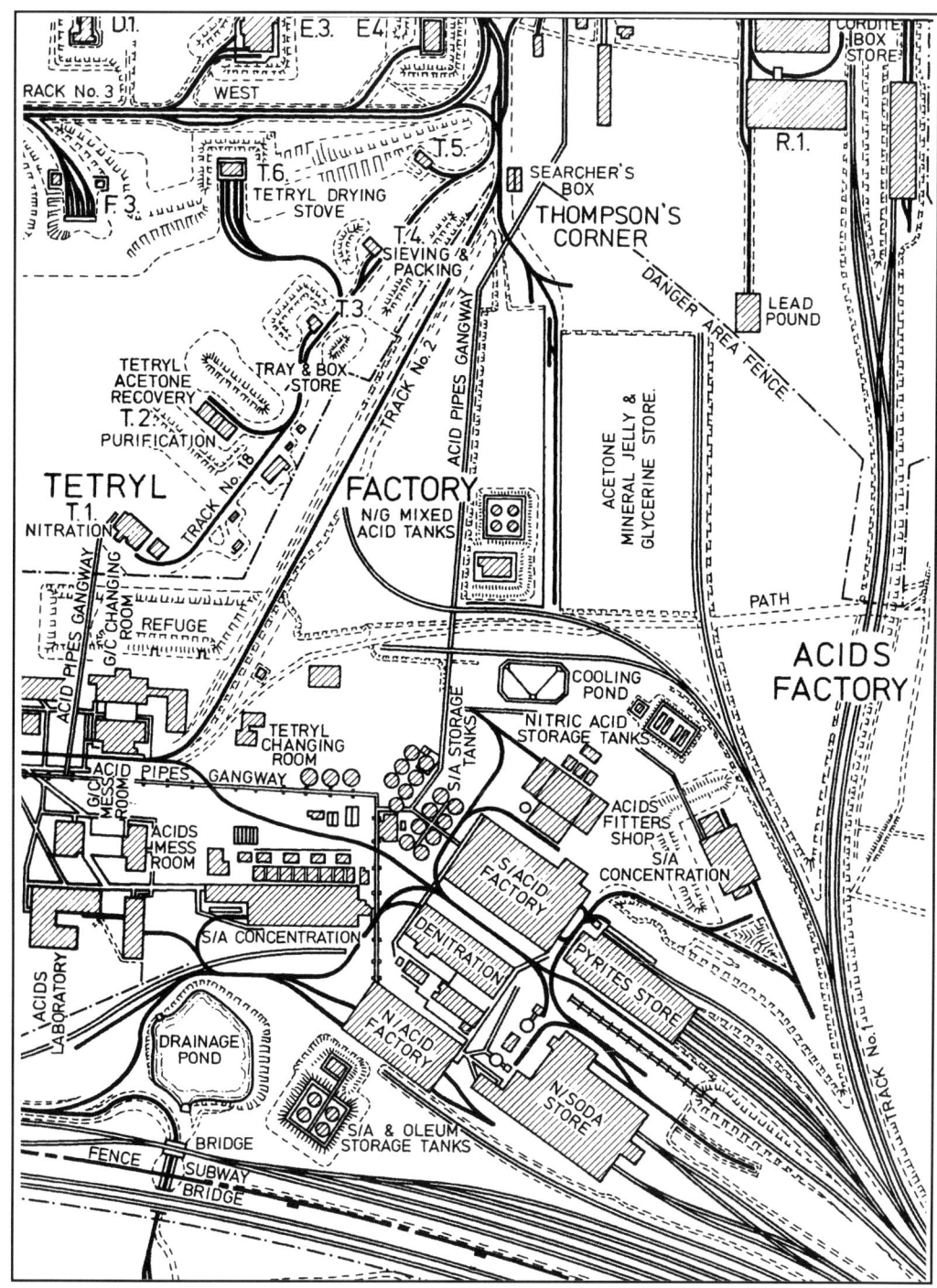

3. Pleasure - Dorset

CREEKMOOR LIGHT RAILWAY

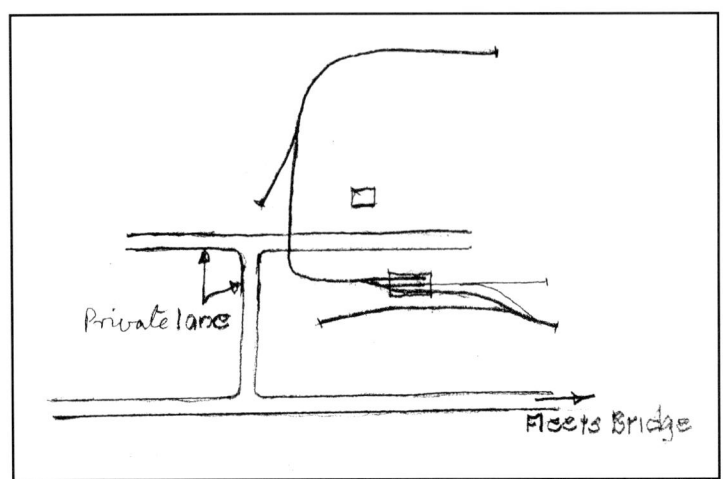

This two-foot gauge line was begun in 1967 and was technically for agricultural transport. It was situated north of the later Upton bypass route and it closed in about mid-1972.

3.1   The track was owned and constructed by Trevor Waterman and was usually operated by 1941 Motor Rail diesel no. 8644 *Druid*. It often carried a headcode disc, which gave the impression of alternative routes. This rural scene was later obliterated by housing. (P.Henshaw)

3.2   The sole steam locomotive was 1921 Orenstein & Koppel 0-6-0WT *Fojo*, which had been imported from Portugal. It was moved to Hertfordshire and renamed *Nantmor*. It went to The Ffestiniog Railway for restoration in January 2005. (P.Henshaw)

3.3   Being a private road, no consent was sought for this level crossing over a public right of way. However, a red target was fitted on a classical white gate. (P.Henshaw)

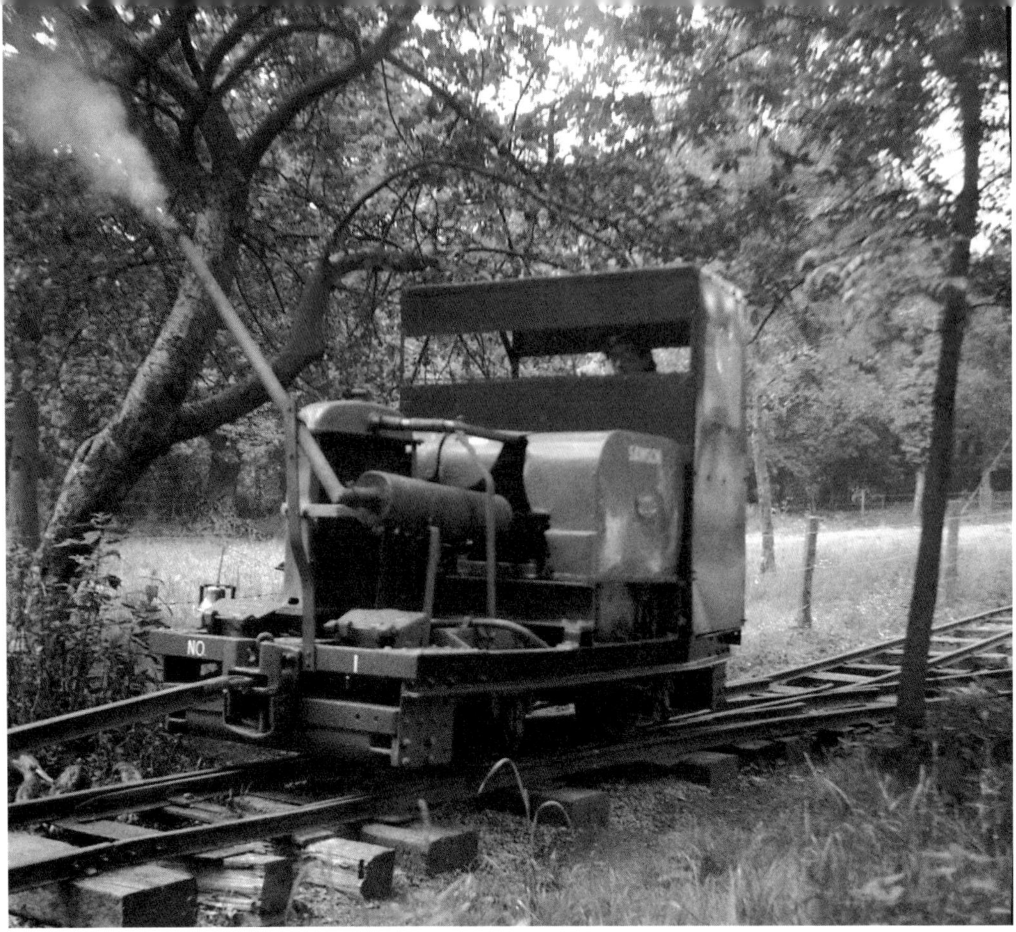
NO. 1

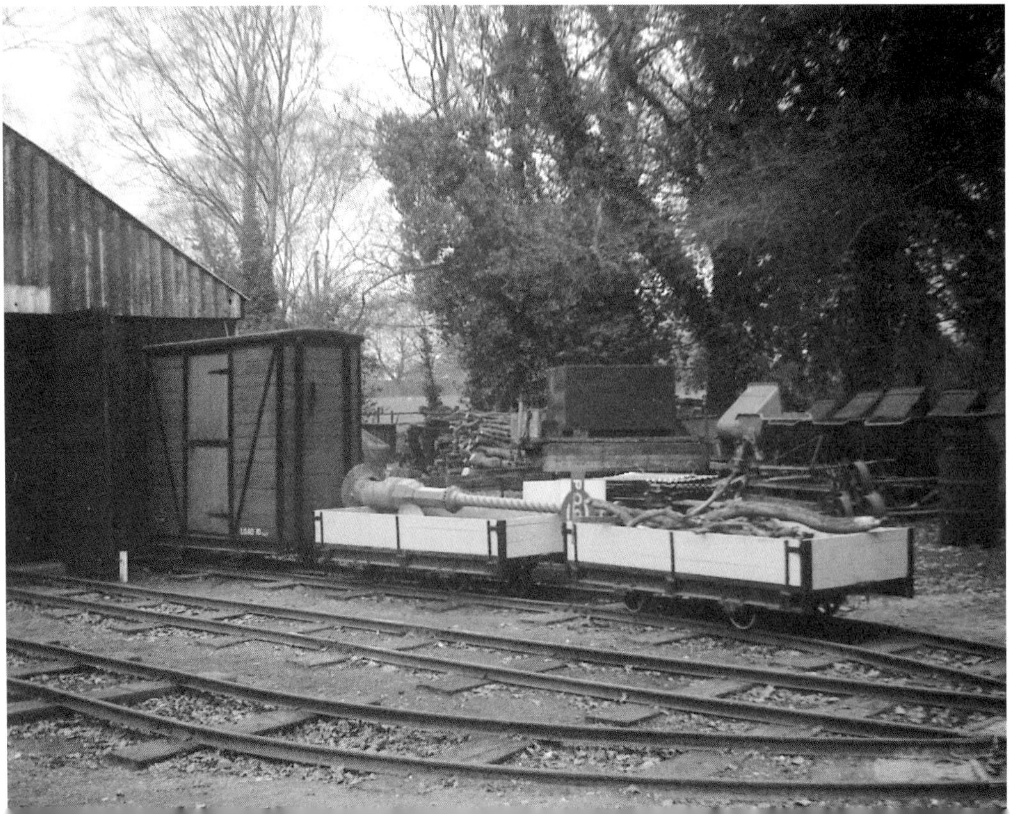

←——— 3.4 Alternative motor power was provided by this Simplex diesel named *Sampson*. There was a similar one called *Odirs*. (P.Henshaw)

←——— 3.5 Not included is the coach, but most of the remainder of the rolling stock is in this photograph. Note the skips in the background. (P.Henshaw)

3.6 The headshunt beyond the coach was so short that it could not accommodate the vehicle. Three point movements were required to turn it prior to entry to the shed. This is the mid-point of the manoeuvre. (P.Henshaw)

CROCKWAY LIGHT RAILWAY

3.7   Much of the track and stock of the Creekmoor line went to Trevor Waterman's Crockway Farm, south of Maiden Newton. A new building was erected and 1936 Ruston diesel no. 179880 arrived from L.W.Vass Ltd of Ampthill. It became no. 3 *Brunel*. (P.Nicholson)

3.8   All photographs are from 29th March 1975 and this one includes the two power units seen at Creekmoor. All the items were sold at auction on 25th October 1979. (P.Nicholson)

3.9   The tall van and bogie coach from Creekmoor saw little use on the grass covered track, which was never extended as planned. It ran between the A356 and the Yeovil to Dorchester line and BR drivers often sounded a greeting with their horns. (P.Nicholson)

PURBECK
MINERAL AND MINING MUSEUM

3.10   *Secundus* has been seen in pictures 1.27, 1.31 and 1.32. It left the closed museum in Birmingham on loan on 22nd January 2004 and went to Herston Locomotive Works at Swanage. It is seen in the museum in Corfe Castle goods shed, where it arrived on 16th March 2004, devoid of its skirt and boiler cladding. The museum also had a clay wagon and a mine tub. (M.Turvey)

3.11   Track was relaid on Skew Bridge at Norden in 2004, as part of an extensive narrow gauge layout to demonstrate the former system. The foreman's hut was the first building to be brought on site. A train waits to return to Swanage from the terminus on 25th April 2004.
(Andrew P.M.Wright)

3.12   No. 7 Mine building at Norden was donated by Imerys Ltd and dismantled after numbering of each component. It is being reassembled near Eldons Siding site on 22nd January 2006 and it would eventually form an important visitor centre. (Andrew P.M.Wright)

TINY TRAMWAY MINING COMPANY
CORFE MULLEN

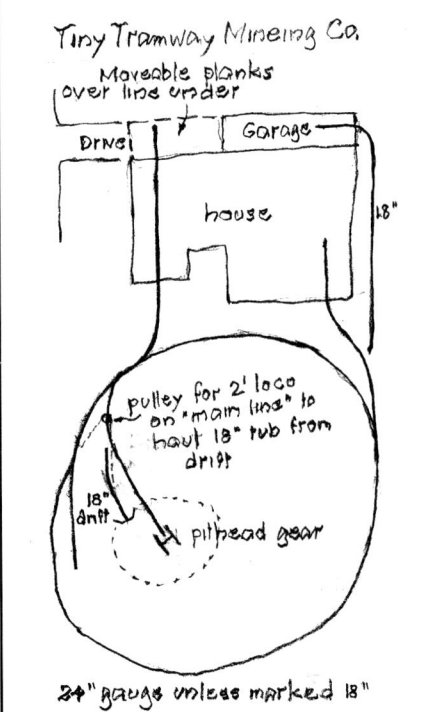

3.13   Pre-dating Fred Dibnah's excavation, Tim Shelton dug a mine shaft in his garden, the pithead gear comprising a motor cycle wheel. Substantial quantities of sand were mined and a drift mine was added. It is on the right of this photograph from January 1992; work had started more than a year earlier. (P.Henshaw)

The site was unorthodox in the extreme; even down to the spelling, as shown on this sketch map. The loading arrangement in the drive allowed lorries to discharge into wagons. (P.Henshaw)

(top right) 3.14   Attached to the Simplex is the chain used for moving stock in and out of the drift mine, although its track gauge was six inches less than the running line. There was also a Clay Cross Lister diesel loco, plus very assorted rolling stock. Most of the items went to Honiton in 1994-95 and the site was developed for housing. (P.Henshaw)

POSTSCRIPT

3.15 "Don't lead me up the garden path" had a new meaning at this secret location in Dorset on 16th April 2005, when Peter Vallins was photographed on his Lister no. 9256 of 1937. It originally had a JAP petrol engine and was last used commercially at Bell House Brickworks in Eastwood, Essex. (P.Nicholson)

4. Industry - Somerset

OAKHILL BREWERY

4.1   Oakhill is a village situated about two miles north of Shepton Mallet and its brewery was unusual in operating a 2ft 6ins gauge (often misquoted as 3ft) line to the nearest railway station, which was at Binegar. Bagnalls supplied this 0-4-0ST new to the railway when it opened in 1904. It was sold to N.Hingley in Netherton in 1920. (J.K.Williams coll.)

4.2   This Peckett 0-4-0ST was also new to Oakhill Brewery in 1904 and was named *Oakhill*. Binegar was on the Somerset & Dorset route and is illustrated in our *Bath to Evercreech Junction* album. The line climbed at 1 in 30 from the brewery; there were three level crossings on the route. (J.K.Williams coll.)

4.3   The other side of *Oakhill* is seen before the line closed in 1921. This engine was sold to the cement works near Penarth illustrated in our *Branch Lines around Barry*. (J.K.Williams coll.)

The line's indirect course is shown on the 1919 edition at 2 ins to 1 mile. The viaduct is at the most northerly road crossing.

COLLIERIES

4.4   Pensford is about half way between Radstock and Bristol; illustrations 72 to 79 in our *Frome to Bristol* album show the station area. There was a two-foot gauge tramway, one mile long, beween Bromley and Pensford Collieries from 1910 to 1957. The rope returns to the left of the train in this August 1956 photograph. Initially, the line was worked by an Avonside 0-4-0T. (C.G.Maggs)

4.5   Pensford Colliery had a standard gauge siding and produced coal until 13th December 1958. The end of the line to Bromley Colliery is seen in the Summer of 1959. It ceased production on 18th May 1957. (M.A.N.Johnston)

4.6   This is Mendip Shaft (formerly Strap Colliery) on 31st July 1967, with part of the 2ft 9ins tub circuit visible. The shaft was 1758ft deep and closed on 28th September 1968. The pit was south of Chilcompton station (S&D) and was linked underground with New Rock Colliery. (M.A.N.Johnston)

4.7   Foxcote Colliery opened in 1859 and much of its output went down an incline to Lower Writhlington Colliery. The remainder went southwards on a 2ft 8½ins gauge tramway to a depot at Turner's Tower. The line received this locomotive from Hudswell Clarke in 1890; coal production ceased in 1931. (E.Haigh)

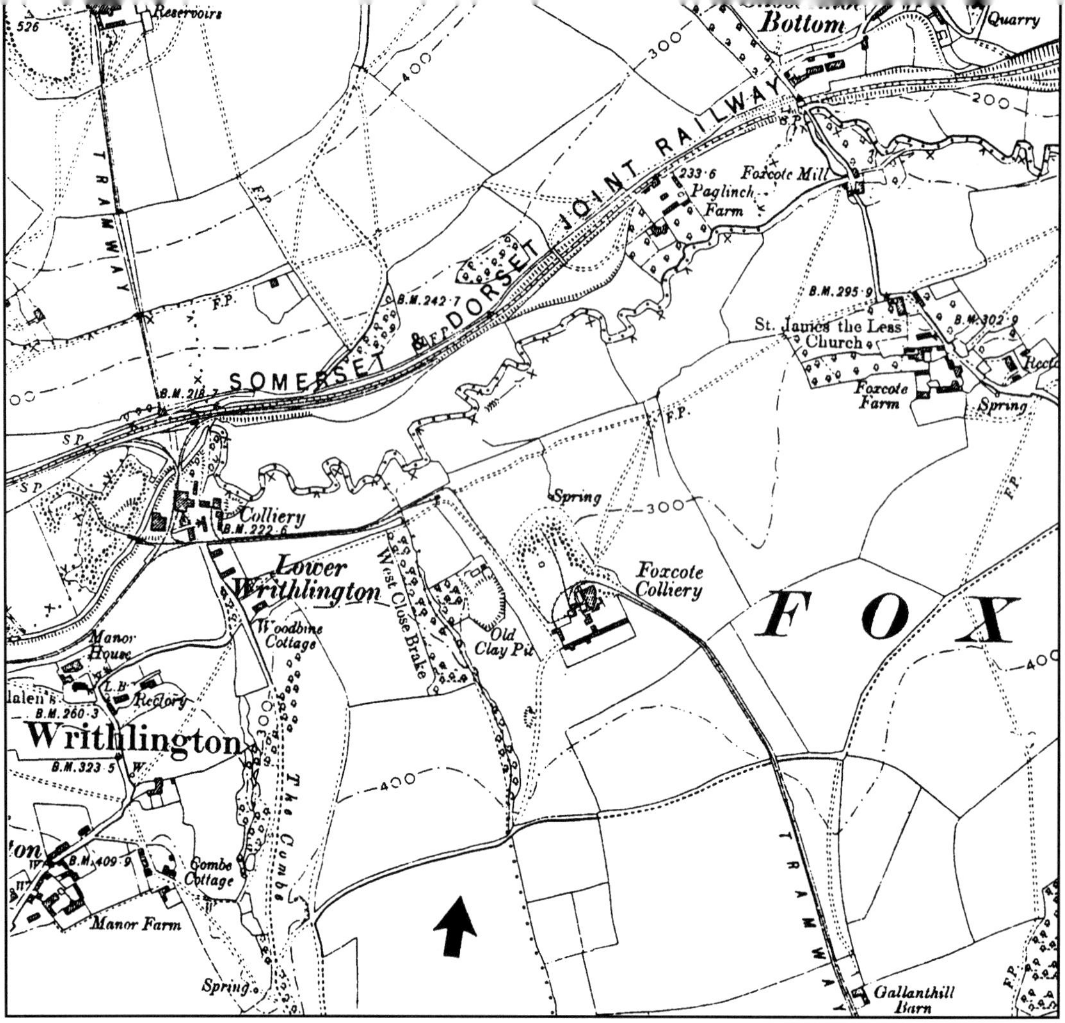

The 6ins to 1 mile map from 1904 has part of the route lower right. Top left is the incline to Braysdown Colliery. Radstock is ½ mile west of Writhlington.

4.8   Kilmersdon Colliery also had 2ft 8½ ins gauge track and this view southwestwards is from August 1960. Closure took place in September 1973. A standard gauge incline was south of Radstock Wagon Works and was one of the last in use in the area. (M.A.N.Johnston)

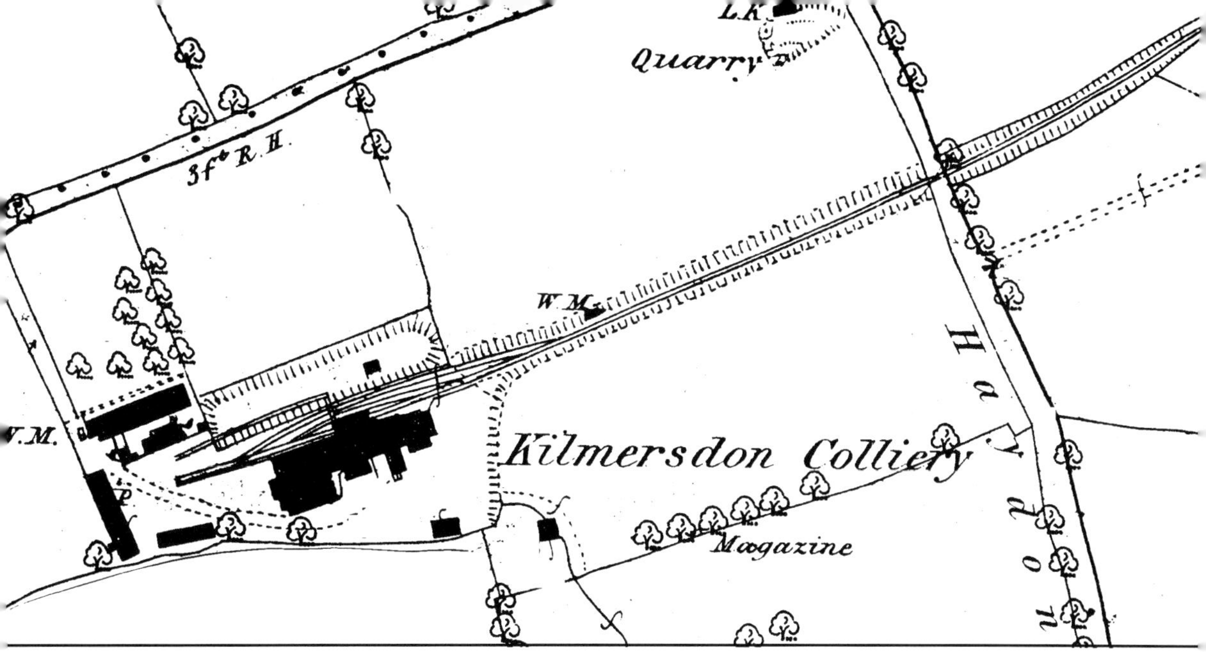

The 1886 survey at 25ins to 1 mile shows the surface narrow gauge in its infancy, with one line on the north side.

4.9   A small section of 2ft 8½ ins gauge track at New Rock Colliery is visible in this 1967 photograph. The pit was near Chilcompton and was in use until 28th September 1968, having been sunk in about 1819. Its shaft depth was 1182 feet. (M.A.N.Johnston)

4.10   Norton Hill Colliery was near Midsomer Norton and its siding can be seen in picture 68 in *Bath to Evercreech Junction*. The 2ft 4ins gauge tracks near the headgear are seen in August 1960; coal production ceased on 11th February 1966. Two compressed air rams for wagon movement are visible. (M.A.N.Johnston)

4.11   Lower Writhlington Colliery was sunk in 1829, but it was not until about 1867 that a 2ft 8½ins line was laid to link it with Upper Writhlington and Foxcote Collieries. Horses were used until about 1882; *Writhlington* arrived new from Hudswell Clarke in 1900. (J.K.Williams coll.)

4.12 Another new locomotive to the line was this 0-4-0ST from Peckett in 1920. There were underground connections to Kilmersdon and Braysdown Collieries. (J.K.Williams coll.)

4.13 A northward view at Lower Writhlington Colliery in August 1960 includes part of the winding house. Closure took place in September 1973 and all evidence was destroyed, as elsewhere in the Somerset Coalfield. The track gauge was 2ft 8½ins. (M.A.N.Johnston)

Huish Colliery was on the opposite side of the valley from Kilmersdon. It was operative from 1824 to 1912 and is shown on the 1880 map, with the narrow gauge lines radiating from the winding house and the GWR Frome-Radstock line on the left.

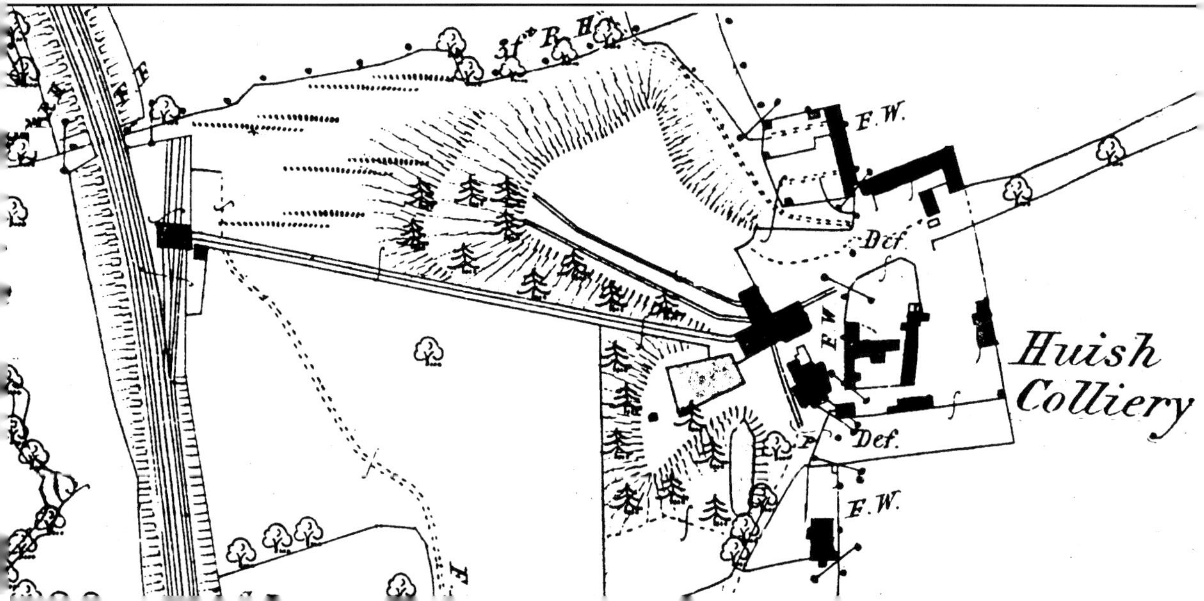

Tyning Colliery
(Disused)

Old Shaft

Limekiln

Chy.

W.T.

Hill

SOMERSET & DORSET JOINT RAILWAY

S.P.

Pump House

Tanks

Filter Beds

C.S.

Sewage Works
(Radstock U.D. Council)

Foot Bridge

Saw Mill

River   S o m e r

ks

3 ft.F.F.

Tennis Court

Def.

3 ft.R.H.

3 ft.R.H.

F.P.

F.P.

3 ft.R.H.

3 ft.R.H.

U.D.Bdy.

3 ft.R.H.

3 ft.R.H.

C.R.

B.P.

384

B.P.

3 ft.F.W.

Mel

Drum

Sls.

S.D.

Hillside

F.B.

Upper Writhlin
Colliery
(Disused)

Sewage Works
(Frome R.D.Council)

Tank

T

R

A

M

W

A

Y

W.M.

F.W.

406   BM 405.34

W.T.

Mount
Pleasant

W.T.

IELD

Allotment
Gardens

Coal Depôt

Seward
Terrace

W.M.

Te
Co

The 1931 survey at 20ins to 1 mile includes a large part of the narrow gauge route across both pages. The pit top left had closed in 1909.

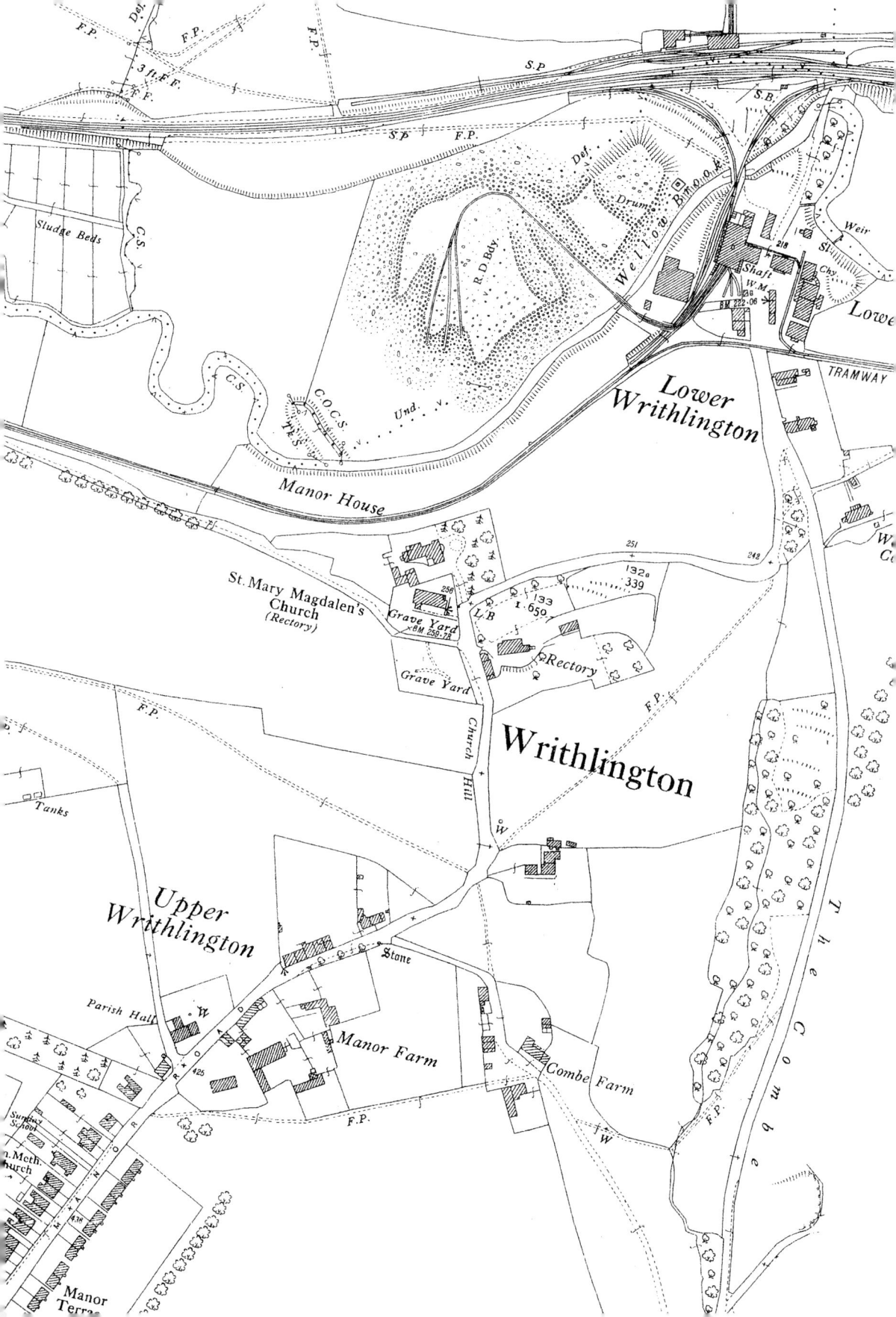

PEAT

4.14   The Eclipse Peat Company's two-foot gauge line crossed the route featured in our *Burnham to Evercreech Junction* album between Shapwick and Ashcott. Picture 70 shows the disastrous collision that took place on this unauthorised crossing on 19th August 1949. (S.C.Nash)

4.15   Fisons Ltd had acquired the business by the time that these two photographs were taken on 19th August 1976. An empty train is crossing South Drain. (M.A.N.Johnston)

4.16 The firm used 13 Lister 4WDMs; the possible dates for the line are 1922-77. Here we are on Shapwick Heath. (M.A.N.Johnston)

4.17 Part of the fleet of Listers was recorded outside the shed at Ashcott on 24th September 1967. (P.Nicholson)

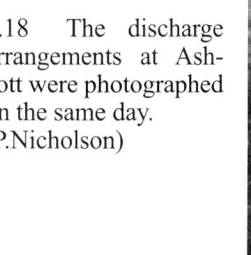

4.18 The discharge arrangements at Ashcott were photographed on the same day. (P.Nicholson)

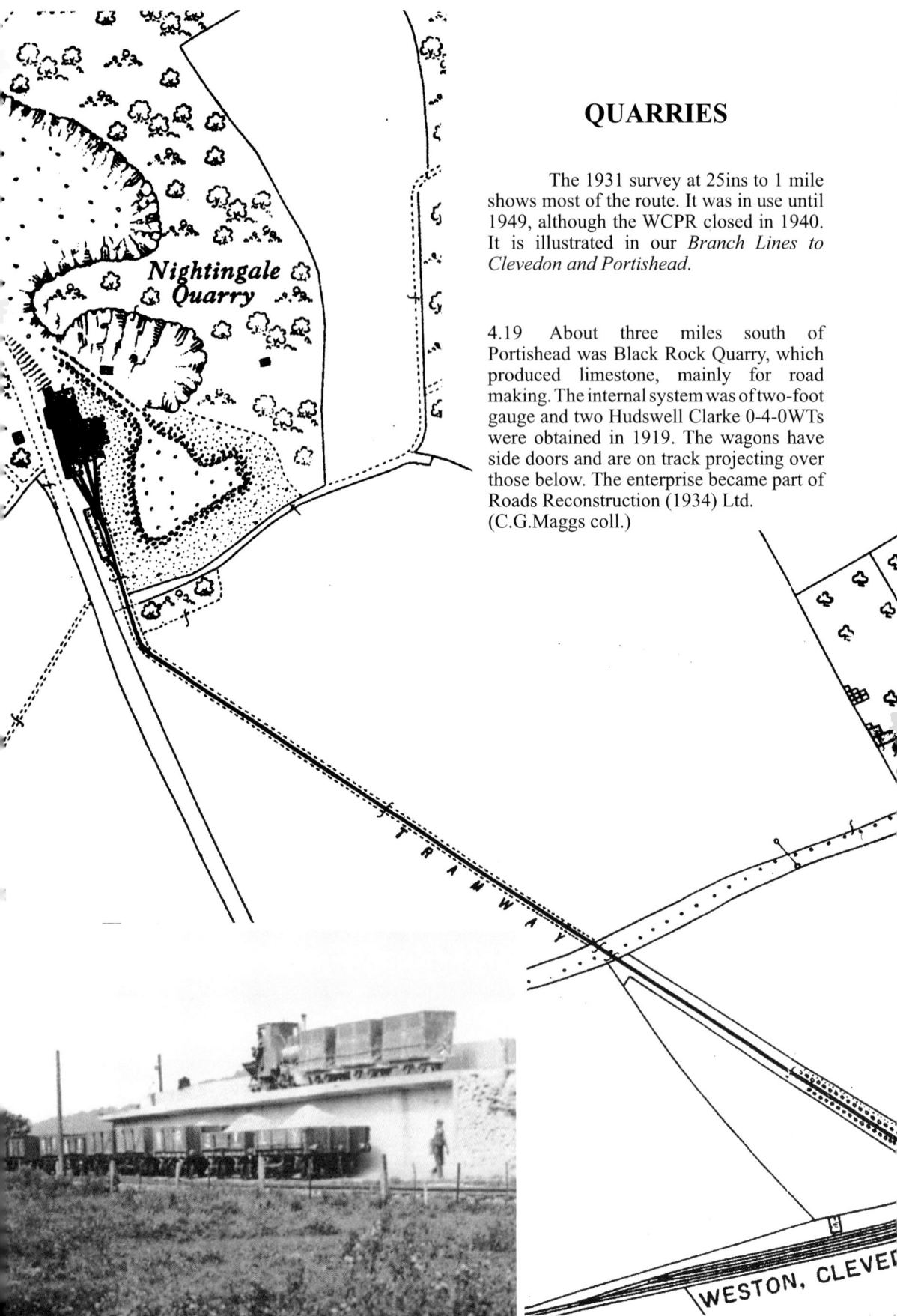

QUARRIES

The 1931 survey at 25ins to 1 mile shows most of the route. It was in use until 1949, although the WCPR closed in 1940. It is illustrated in our *Branch Lines to Clevedon and Portishead*.

4.19 About three miles south of Portishead was Black Rock Quarry, which produced limestone, mainly for road making. The internal system was of two-foot gauge and two Hudswell Clarke 0-4-0WTs were obtained in 1919. The wagons have side doors and are on track projecting over those below. The enterprise became part of Roads Reconstruction (1934) Ltd. (C.G.Maggs coll.)

Nightingale Quarry

TRAMWAY

WESTON, CLEVED

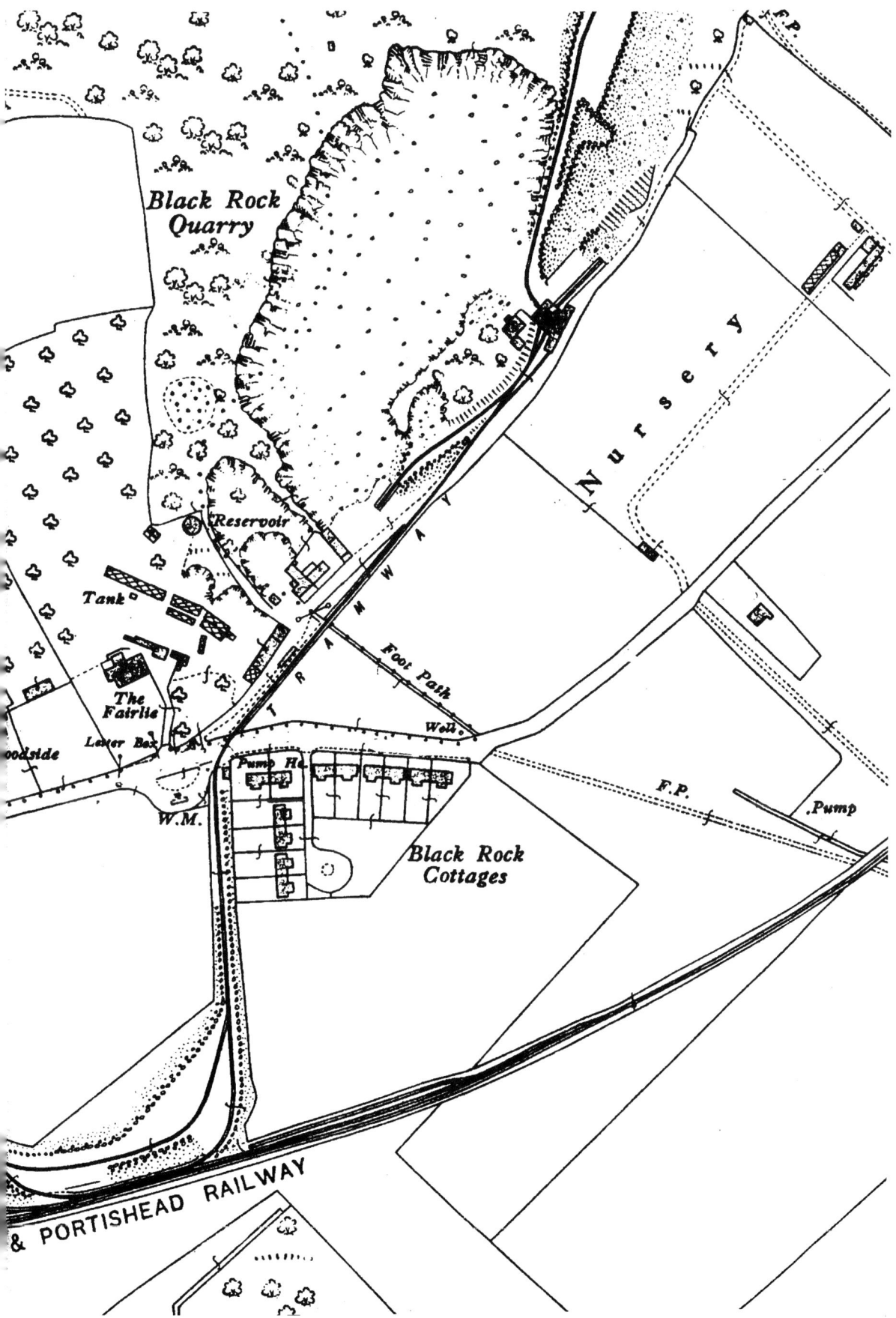

4.20 Peckett supplied 0-4-0ST *Gamecock* new in 1904 to the Somerset Basalt Quarry Company's Downhead Quarry. It passed to Roads Reconstruction Ltd when the quarry closed in about 1925. The system was two-foot gauge. (J.K.Williams coll.)

4.21 The Cranmore plant depot of Roads Reconstruction (1934) Ltd was on the site of the former Waterling Quarry of the Mendip Granite & Asphalt Co. Ltd, and Kerr Stuart 0-4-2ST no. 3065 of 1918 was photographed there in 1950. It was ex-Air Ministry, Eastleigh Aerodrome, around 1920 and worked at New Frome Quarry, until about 1948. (J.K.Williams coll.)

4.22 Photographed at the same time was 0-4-0T Avonside Engine Company no. 2073 of 1933. It had been supplied new to Durham County Water Board as no. 85 *Sunderland* and had come via Grovesend Quarry, Gloucestershire in April 1949. It was sent to India in about 1951. (J.K.Williams coll.)

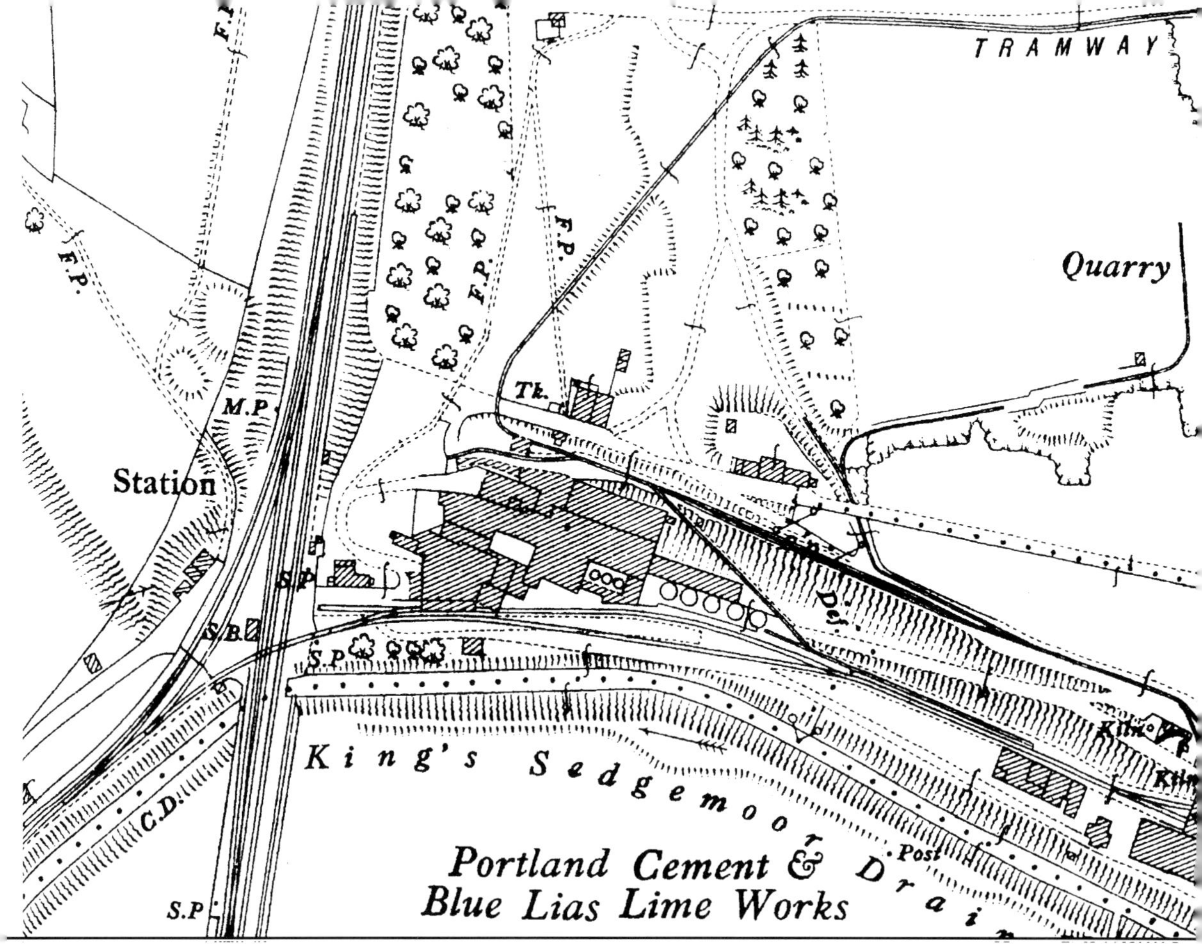

Dunball was the location of this works, which was connected to Dunball Wharf by the lines on the left. The station and junction are illustrated in our *Taunton to Bristol* album. The 25ins to 1 mile map is from 1930 and had the two-foot gauge lines north of the works.

4.23   John Board & Co. Ltd purchased this 1915 Kerr Stuart 0-4-2T secondhand for use between the works and Dunball Quarry. The works closed in 1954. (J.K.Williams coll.)

4.24   The West Somerset Mineral Railway was standard gauge and ran south from the Minehead branch at Watchet. It was completed in 1863 and closed in 1898, but was reopened briefly in part by the Somerset Mineral Syndicate Ltd from 1907 to 1910. Eight miles from Watchet is Brendon Hill from where this two-foot gauge line ran east to an iron ore mine at Colton. The loco is a Bagnall 0-4-0WT, thought to be no. 300 of 1880, and is pictured on the short timber viaduct, some eight feet high, opposite Raleigh's Cottages. (J.K.Williams coll.)

5. Pleasure - Somerset

GARTELL LIGHT RAILWAY

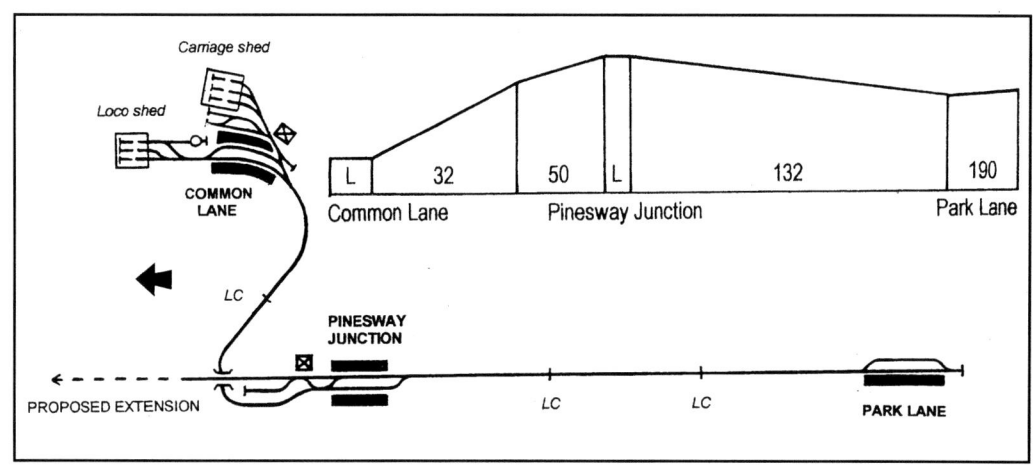

John Gartell purchased some two-foot gauge equipment from Fisons on the Somerset Levels in 1984. He planned a short line near his house in Common Lane, Yenston, one mile southeast of Templecombe station. The track was eventually extended to pass under, and climb onto, the trackbed of the former Somerset & Dorset Railway, featured in our *Bournemouth to Evercreech Junction* album. It is represented by the straight line along the bottom of this 2005 diagram.

5.1   The first open day was held in 1990 and this shows the simple engine shed and the optimistic headboard at the second one, in the following year. The locomotive is Lister DM 0-4-0 no. 1 *Amanda*. The name was later transferred to a new engine. (P.G.Barnes)

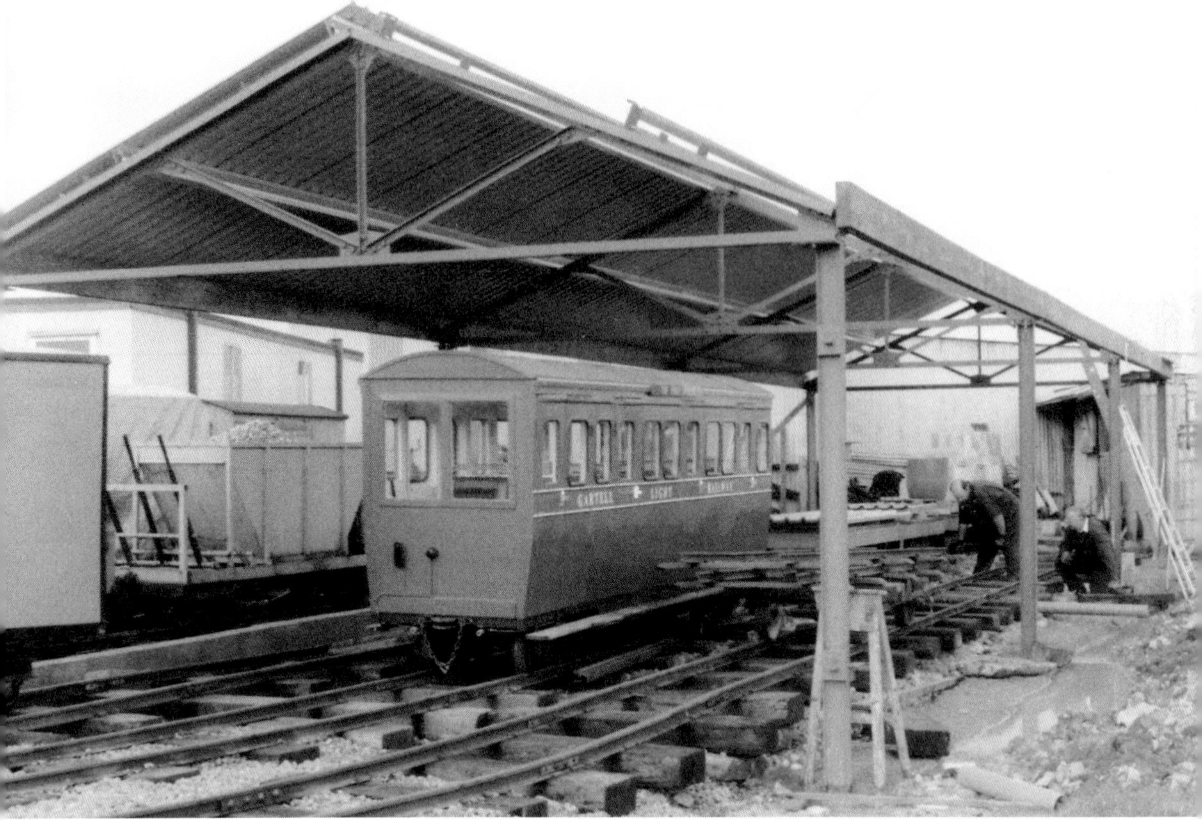

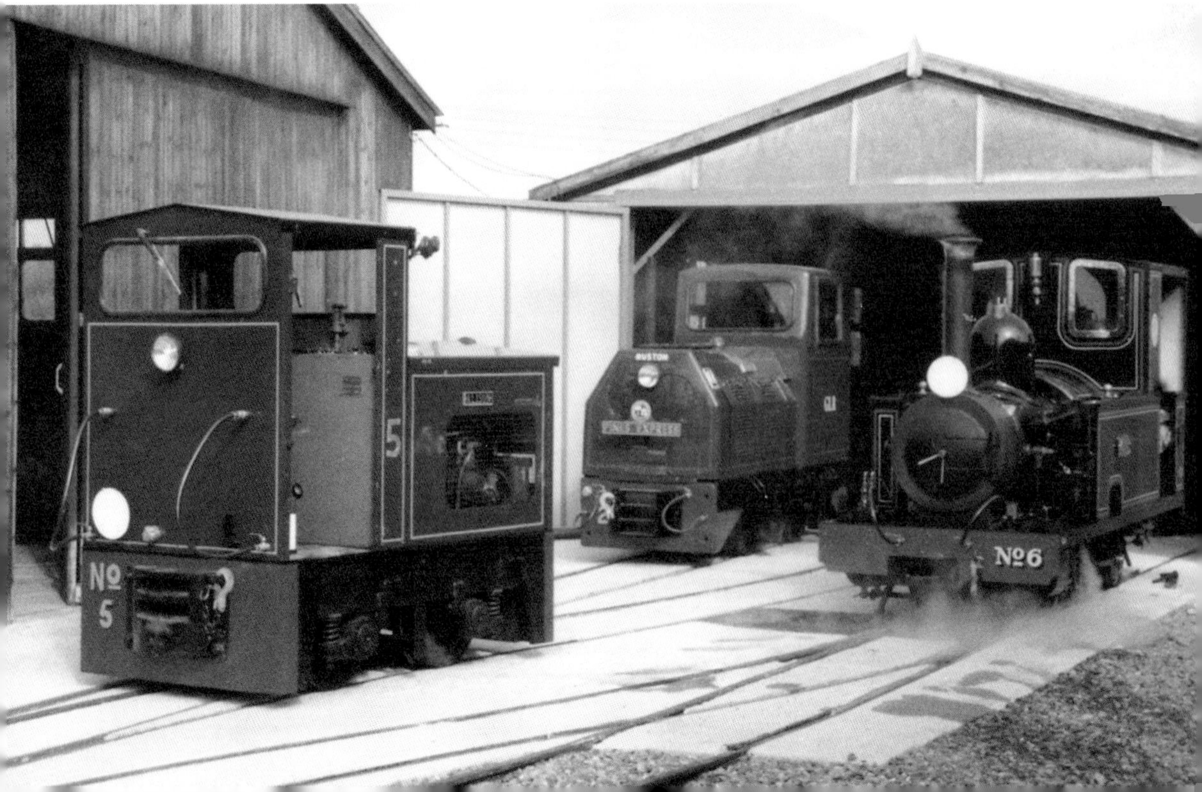

5
No 5
No6

5.2   Development continued unabated and this splendid carriage shed was recorded under construction in 1999. Fine workmanship is also evident in one of the fleet of nine coaches and the useful ballast hopper wagon is also to be seen. (M.Lucas)

5.3   The layout outside the shed shown in picture 5.1 was altered greatly in 2000 and is seen in 2002 with diesel hydraulic no. 5 *Alison*, Ruston diesel hydraulic no. 2 *Andrew* carrying the Pines Express headboard and 0-4-2T no. 6 *Mr G*. The latter was completed in 1998 by the North Dorset Locomotive Works, at Motcombe near Shaftesbury. (G.Baseden)

5.4   An early view of Common Lane taken from the footbridge shows the rudimentary platform 1 constructed from pre-cast concrete sections. Apart from the two enclosed coaches (like all the GLR's enclosed coaches, these were built on site in the company's own well-equipped workshops), the signal box and the lamp standard on platform 2, everything else here has changed beyond recognition since this picture was taken in the early 1990s. (I.Matthews)

COMMON LANE
COMMON LANE

GARTELL LIGHT RAILWAY
ENGINEERING DEPARTMENT
G L R

←——— 5.5   The spacious new station complex at Common Lane, which houses the buffet, ticket office and toilets - and doubles as a function suite with seating for up to 200 - is visible in the background as Bo-Bo diesel hydraulic no. 1 *Amanda*, propels its train out of platform 1 before drawing forward into platform 2 with the next departure for Park Lane. On most open days, an intensive 3-train service is operated, with departures every 15 minutes from 10.30 until the last train of the day at 16.30. (M.Lucas)

←——— 5.6   The GLR works train stands on the S&D alignment on 4th May 1998 on the bridge built over the line from the terminus. There is also a well wagon for conveyance of a mechanical digger. (P.Henshaw)

5.7   Lister diesel mechanical no. 1 *Amanda* approaches Pinesway station, as it was known in the summer of 1994, with the down Pines Express. The original 7-lever signal box was still in use, although work had already started on its replacement. All thirty of the levers in the ex-Becton Gasworks frame in the new box would be needed on completion of the northern extension of the line. (M.Lucas)

5.8   Pinesway Junction station is seen from the south, showing a remarkable array of semaphore signals. Visible in the foreground is the experimental track panel, which was laid in 2003 using concrete sleepers manufactured on site. (M.Lucas)

5.9   At Park Lane, the GLR's southern terminus, there is a run-round loop controlled by a 5-lever ground frame, here being operated by the guard. The section between Park Lane and Pinesway Junction is worked by token. (G.Baseden)

standard gauge

→ N

unfinished one mile

woods

barn

VOBSTER
LIGHT RAILWAY

This sketch from 1994 indicates the extent of the development, the dashes showing the unfinished length.

The location was south of Mells Road station and is shown on a diagram produced in 1995. It also shows many of the earlier narrow gauge lines in the area of the Newbury Railway. Mells Road station is illustrated in pictures 25-28 in our *Frome to Bristol* album.

RADSTOCK

MELLS ROAD

Asphaltic Limestone Concrete Co Ltd

NEWBURY RAILWAY

Jericho Bridge

MELLS QUARRIES RAILWAY

Mells Cly

VOBSTER LIGHT RAILWAY 2'

Holwell Farm

Old Newbury Cly

up Newbury Cly

ckintosh incline

tramroad 2'4"

engine shed

NEWBURY RAILWAY

Vobster Quarry

2' tramroad
Catch Cly

limekiln

tunnel

2' tramroad
Bilbao Quarry

Bilbao Cly

VOBSTER CROSS

MELLS

BURY Goodeaves Cly

EFORD

VOBSTER CROSS ?

up
incline

VOBSTER

:::::::DORSET & SOMERSET CANAL

R.F.Newman

Vobster Breach Cly

Vobster Cly Vobster Old Cly

coke ovens 2' tramroad

0 ¼m ½m ¾m 1m

5.10   A barn at Holwell Farm was the base for this enthusiast's enterprise and is seen on 13th December 1992; it housed two sidings. Track laying had begun about 12 months earlier. (P.Henshaw)

5.11   By the time that this photograph was taken on the second open day on 4th July 1993, the line had reached the trackbed of the Newbury Railway, which had earlier served 15 small collieries and several quarries, the last of the latter closing in 1959. The locomotive stock comprised two Rustons and a Simplex, but by mid-1994 all the equipment had been dispersed. The plan had been to have an interchange at Mells Road. (P.Henshaw)

RADSTOCK LIGHT RAILWAY

5.12 Much of the equipment from the Vobster Light Railway was moved to the Somerset & Avon Railway Association's site at Radstock and this is the scene on the Open Day on 23rd April 1995. In addition to the two diesels from Vobster, a large 48hp Ruston & Hornsby diesel (left) was present. The former Radstock Wagon Works was used as a base to launch a scheme to revive the railway southwards, but consent was still awaited ten years later. However, a narrow gauge line in the area seemed even less likely. (P.Nicholson)

WESTONZOYLAND

5.13 The Westonzoyland Pumping Station Trust was established to preserve the pumps on the Somerset Levels, near Bridgwater. Other pumps have been added for display and a two-foot gauge demonstration has been included. It did carry passengers for a period, until bureaucracy overwhelmed it. Seen on 20th April 2003 are Motor Rail no. 405310 of 1968 and Lister no. 34758 of 1949, ex-Fisons. Surplus wagons went to another demonstration line, near Washford station on the West Somerset Railway. (P.Nicholson)

MP Middleton Press

EVOLVING THE ULTIMATE RAIL ENCYCLOPEDIA

Easebourne Lane, Midhurst, West Sussex.
GU29 9AZ   Tel:01730 813169

www.middletonpress.co.uk   email:info@middletonpress.co.uk

A-0 906520   B-1 873793   C-1 901706   D-1 904474

OOP Out of Print at time of printing - Please check current availability   **BROCHURE AVAILABLE SHOWING NEW TITLES**